CW00762481

Witches an

Studies in Public and Applied Anthropology

General Editors: **Sarah Pink**, RMIT University, Melbourne, Australia, and **Simone Abram**, Durham University and Leeds Beckett University

The value of anthropology to public policy, business and third sector initiatives is increasingly recognized, not least due to significant innovations in the discipline. The books published in this series offer important insight into these developments by examining the expanding role of anthropologists practicing their discipline outside academia as well as exploring the ethnographic, methodological and theoretical contribution of anthropology, within and outside academia, to issues of public concern.

Witches and Demons

A Comparative Perspective on Witchcraft and Satanism

Jean La Fontaine

berghahn
NEW YORK · OXFORD
www.berghahnbooks.com

Published in 2016 by
Berghahn Books
www.berghahnbooks.com

Library of Congress Cataloging-in-Publication Data
Names: La Fontaine, J. S. (Jean Sybil), 1931– author.
Title: Witches and demons: a comparative perspective on witchcraft and
    Satanism / Jean La Fontaine.
Description: New York: Berghahn Books, [2016] | Includes bibliographical
references and index.
Identifiers: LCCN 2015045572 | ISBN 9781785330858 (hardback: alk. paper) |
    ISBN 9781785331527 (pbk.: alk. paper) | ISBN 9781785330865 (ebook)
Subjects: LCSH: Witchcraft. | Good and evil. | Demonology.
Classification: LCC BF1566 .L3 2016 | DDC 133.409--dc23 LC record available at
http://lccn.loc.gov/2015045572

British Library Cataloguing in Publication Data
A catalogue record for this book is available from the British Library

ISBN 978-1-78533-085-8 hardback
ISBN 978-1-78533-152-7 paperback
ISBN 978-1-78533-086-5 ebook

CONTENTS

ACKNOWLEDGEMENTS

These articles have emerged from papers and lectures delivered to many university departments, primarily in anthropology and the sociology of religion and edited, where necessary, to bring them up to date. I am happy to thank the following institutions for their invitations and for the stimulating discussions of my material that ensued: the universities of New Hampshire, USA (The Saul Sidore Memorial Lecture), Amsterdam, St Andrews, Sussex, University College London and the Institute for Anthropological Research in Africa of the University of Leuven in Brussels. One chapter – on children and evil – was the result of time spent as Visiting Professor in Tema Barn, the institute for research on children at Linkoping University, Sweden; although not based on any particular paper it owes a good deal to papers and seminars I gave there and on visits to the anthropology department of the University of Copenhagen. My warm thanks to both institutions for their hospitality. Two other chapters are revised versions of published articles and I am grateful to the editors of the journal *Etnofoor*, published by the University of Amsterdam, and to INFORM and their publishers, Ashgate, for permission to reprint these, albeit in somewhat revised versions. I must also thank the Metropolitan Police for permission to read cases in their archives; I hope my report on them, on which an additional chapter was based, was useful.

I benefitted greatly from the reviews of the two readers of my manuscript; I thank them both. I enjoyed several useful discussions with Dr Joost Fontein of the court case we were both associated with. Finally, I particularly wish to thank Amanda Sackur who rescued me from the becalmed doldrums of revision, enabling me to rewrite the Introduction. Many thanks also to my grandson, Kwami Odoom, for constructing the index.

Berghahn's editorial staff have been a pleasure to work with: so quick to respond and so patient with my delays! Thank you.

My family has always been a source of comfort and support; I dedicate this book to them all with my love.

Jean La Fontaine

INTRODUCTION
Understanding the Other

Devil worship, black magic and witchcraft are the subjects of discussion in this book. The approach that informs them shows its anthropological nature in three basic elements. First, in various ways the chapters all display the comparative method, the long-accepted means by which anthropology has drawn conclusions about particular societies, tested generalisations and theories against this ethnography and thus contributed to the body of theories that explain society in a general sense. Secondly, they consider the anthropologist's perpetual problem, which is that they are members of a particular society themselves and cannot entirely divest themselves of its ways of thinking and feeling in order to achieve the neutral, unbiased approach to their material that is the profession's ideal. Despite themselves, they may distort their understanding of their subject matter by an ethnocentric attitude to the other societies they study. Finally, the chapters share a subject matter that exemplifies culturally shaped but changeable ideas and behaviour, and the way in which both of these react to the social, political and economic background that forms their context.

It is well known that anthropological research has long been based on comparisons, which sets ethnographic descriptions beside each other in order first to understand the individual societies, and second to contribute to more general and abstract theories of society. The comparative method has characterised the subject since its inception and has been accepted as a parallel to the scientific methods being developed in other branches of knowledge. Indeed it is described by Peel as Anthropology's Charter (forthcoming). Durkheim was an early example; he called the comparative method 'the only one suited to sociology' (Durkheim (1895) 1938: 125),[1] by which he meant all social sciences. Half a century later, Goody wrote: 'comparison is an essential means of testing propositions and theories about mankind' (Goody 1969: 8; see also Fortes 1953: 130).

Comparison was first used by the evolutionists to construct a hypothetical development of social man, but when later their theory was rejected, the method was not. Since then it has been used by proponents of a variety of theories in anthropology that differ from each other, making clear the independence of this method from any determination by the character of the theories that were based on using it. The comparative method has continued to support anthropological work since then, but the collection of data for it has been much developed since its original use in the nineteenth century. In particular, research in the field was introduced and is now essential to it.[2] One of the earliest to use field research in the study of witchcraft was Evans-Pritchard (1937) It was only his daily observations among the Azande that allowed him to draw the important conclusion that 'the Zande actualises these beliefs rather than intellectualises them, and their tenets are expressed in socially controlled behaviour rather than in doctrines' (ibid.: 82–83). He thus initiated a whole new approach to ethnographic research by making clear that observation of behaviour as well as information about the ideas that motivated it was necessary to understand other societies, and in particular their concept of witchcraft. Beliefs must be studied in action and in context. Today this precept may sometimes be ignored, to the detriment of the analyses concerned. In the chapters that follow, the importance of the relation of action to ideas will become clear.

Research in the field has faced some anthropologists with serious dilemmas as a result of the confrontation between their own modes of thought and those they are studying. Gilbert Lewis, a medical doctor as well as an anthropologist, called his account of the terminal illness of Dauwaras, a New Guinea villager, 'A Failure of Treatment'. His medical knowledge and that of the local clinic could not account for, or cure, this fatal illness (Lewis 2000: 99–101), which the villagers attributed to several different malevolent spiritual forces.[3] The death left Lewis with a sense of failure, and he wrote: 'Some of the insights came out of interactions which were not easy or uncontested. The question of how far to go [in intervening] was occasionally distressing, for example in cases where I thought (or think) about things that could have been avoided or should not have happened. That question, sadly, hangs over Dauwaras's illness and his death' (ibid.: 16).

Some years later in South Africa, a totally different social context, Isak Niehaus (2013) observed his Western-educated research assistant and friend, Jimmy Mohale, gradually come to believe that what they both knew was AIDS had been inflicted on him by the witchcraft of his father (2013: 163, 168). Despite Niehaus urging him to seek Western medical treatment, he refused and eventually died. It is clear that, like Lewis, Niehaus felt the pain of an outcome that was, to in his eyes, unnecessary. The situations of these two anthropologists, perhaps more extreme than those of others who have reflected on beliefs in magic as they have encountered it, derived from the intimacy of research in the field. Both anthropologists, however, retain their own culture's thinking, and this inability to adopt local understandings of the events adds an extra poignancy to their feelings.

The experiences of these anthropologists would seem to confirm the view that 'Witchcraft is a notion so foreign to us that it is hard for us to appreciate … convictions about its reality' (Evans-Pritchard 1937: 540). Similar statements of unbelief have been made repeatedly over the years that followed (for example: Middleton and Winter 1963: 1; Douglas 1970: xxxiv; Macfarlane 1985, pb. 1989: 57). Recently, however, there have been suggestions that some anthropologists have come close to believing that witchcraft was an empirical reality (Favret-Saada 1980 and Stoll and Olkes 1987 cited by Niehaus), but it has not been argued that witchcraft cannot be understood without accepting the validity of its tenets.[4] On the contrary, Niehaus has stated that 'believing is not a prerequisite for understanding' (2013: 21–22) and clearly both he and Lewis understood the beliefs of the communities in which they were involved. What is being said is that it is possible to take a detached view of the beliefs of other societies and still come to a complete understanding of them.

It is also general knowledge that in the past beliefs in witchcraft did characterise European societies. Historians point out that they did not completely die out until the end of the nineteenth century although the incidence of accusations declined greatly (Thomas 1970: 70). One response to the apparent absence of modern material on Western beliefs to compare with beliefs in witchcraft is thus to go back three hundred or more years and use material on the witch beliefs and witch-hunts of the early modern period.[5] A conference held by the Association of Social Anthropologists in 1968 brought historians and anthropologists together for the first time to consider such a comparison.[6] Thereafter, historians began to use anthropological theories of witchcraft to illuminate their own material, with which comparisons were also made by anthropologists subsequently (see essays by Brown, Cohn, Macfarlane and Thomas, in Douglas 1970).[7] By comparing members of these twentieth-century societies with the communities of three hundred years earlier they were in fact close to confirming the view of evolutionists that magic was primitive thought which was superseded by religion (Frazer 1922) or by science (Tylor 1871).

When the juxtaposition of magic with science or religion was first used it was to demonstrate the superior intellectual claims of the latter and to show that an evolutionary distance separated 'modern' thinking from such erroneous beliefs as were found in 'primitive' society. Levy-Bruhl in his early writings (e.g. 1920) supported the idea that magic exemplified 'primitive thinking' which was 'pre-logical'. Evans-Pritchard's demonstration[8] that the Azande thought quite logically, although on some questions they started from different assumptions, was written in part to refute this view. Today, despite changes in theoretical approaches, the passage of centuries may still be ignored in order to compare the similarities between the witch-hunting in the past of Europe and the witchcraft in the present of other countries without taking into account the passage of time, with its changes to the context of both. Among the public in general, the relegation of belief in witchcraft to 'superstition' continues to come close to classing it as 'primitive'.[9]

The first historical comparisons were flawed by the selection for comparison of only those features of past European culture that seem to resemble, in their form, witch beliefs in the (much later) Third World. In those early studies, (the Christian) religion was excluded from consideration. Thus, in his discussion of 'The Relevance of Social Anthropology to the Historical Study of English Witchcraft', the historian Keith Thomas argued that the concept of the Devil as the god of witches was never central to English ideas, although he also acknowledged that an accusation of witchcraft might be perceived as one of Devil worship '"by interested lawyers or clergy" (Thomas 1970: 49). Nevertheless he explicitly excluded these ideas that derived from contemporary Christianity, which were more wide-spread in Europe, in order to distinguish witchcraft from religion (ibid.). His argument, detailed elsewhere (1973), was that both witchcraft and magic were superseded by the development of medicine, law and the Church that offered more effective solutions to individual problems of illness, misfortune, wrongdoing or conflict.

Later historians of the witch-hunts such as Ankarloo and Henningsen (1990) established that it was not the spread of rational thinking – that is, a change in intellectual culture, or the advent of 'science' – that ended the witch-hunts, but the actions of the authorities, both of Church and State (see Henningsen 1980). It was the Church that had spread the belief that the wise men and women who offered healing charms and other magical answers to common village problems were in fact the servants of Satan and worshipped him in secret rituals that included the most abhorred of crimes. It was also in its power to bring an end to the search for these and other 'witches', which eventually it did, though slowly and piecemeal. In this the Church was supported by the political authorities who finally ended the hunts.[10]

Historians such as Norman Cohn had already criticised the comparisons that had been drawn between the present and the past. In his essay in the volume edited by Mary Douglas (1970), Cohn states: 'At the heart of this fantasy [of witchcraft] is the figure of Satan himself'. He shows how malleable the fantasy has been and how it was *quite different from* [my italics], and vastly more lethal than, the witchcraft beliefs that anthropologists find and study in primitive societies today' (ibid.).[11] European witchcraft is distinguished from most other similar beliefs by the fact that Church and State were not only involved in the hunt for witches but introduced the ideas that inspired and justified it.

The comparison between the European witch-hunts and the witch beliefs of Africa, New Guinea and what is now Latin America, was, in fact, artificially created by ignoring the role of Church and State. It was based on only one aspect of the beliefs in witchcraft that were part of Europe's culture at that time, those that were characteristic of the villages. This was done in order to show their comparability with manifestations in other parts of the world, but the village beliefs did not cause the witch-hunts. They were encouraged by the authorities who linked devil worship with the village beliefs, and forced confessions that confirmed this association.[12] Similarly, as will be shown in the second half of this volume, the influence of Christian doctrine has encouraged the hunt for witches in the twenty-first century; Chapter 8 demonstrates how this may happen.

The idea that magic and science are mutually incompatible is no longer important in modern anthropological thinking. The conviction that science itself is somehow culture-free and totally rational has also been seriously undermined. The work of Thomas Kuhn (1962) established that scientific research itself is a social activity and subject to the influence of the social structure of the research community. Theoretical conclusions established by the research of its senior members are accepted as orthodoxy until the challenge to them becomes sufficiently strong to undermine their position.[13] Nevertheless, differences between religious or magical thinking and science remain: in particular, a challenge to orthodoxy in science is not unthinkable nor a reason to exclude the challenger from the scientific community, and, secondly, the strength of major theoretical conclusions still depends on the evidence supporting them. Spiritual dogmas are not based on evidence in this way, but on faith, and are not thought to be subject to change like scientific theories; the ideas in magic and witchcraft do not form an orthodoxy, although they are generally shared within a community, but they are not subject to challenge on the basis of new evidence. Nevertheless the nature of faith can also be shown to be subject to alteration, as changes in modern witchcraft beliefs documented in several chapters in this book will show.

Over the years since Evans-Pritchard published his classic monograph, anthropologists have studied occult beliefs in the field, recording a mass of ethnographic data on witchcraft, magic and sorcery in their field research, which has allowed them to explain it. They have documented the patterns of accusations, the political, economic and domestic conflicts from which they derive, the relationships that are most liable to such conflict and, latterly, the symbolism in which the fundamental ideas supporting the beliefs are expressed. It has become clear that a full understanding of these beliefs depends on considerable knowledge of the society, its structure and culture. Beliefs in witchcraft are no longer treated as though they were discrete objects in a cultural storehouse, easily extracted to interpret and compare with other beliefs as though they were discrete units of culture. The amount of detail needed for a satisfactory analysis of a single society results in some practical problems in engaging in comparisons. It is now difficult to attempt a cross-cultural comparison that is wider, let alone global, in scope. Hence anthropologists have tended to discard such comparisons.

Attempts made in the past to undertake the broadest comparisons display some of the problems that prevent success in this endeavour. A very early example was that of Sir James Frazer's *The Golden Bough* (first published in 1890), which produced a compendium of similarities and differences, relying heavily on classical sources, but without what today would be considered a sufficient understanding of their cultural significance or context. In such an approach, conclusions drawn from one example become a yardstick for all such beliefs; similarities are noted and differences fade into the background. A single feature becomes the 'cause' of witchcraft accusations or beliefs. Such a single-issue focus allows much broader comparison across a large number of societies but the result wrongly implies that the aspect considered is the only relevant one. To take a modern example, if an accusation of witchcraft is the end result of rumour and gossip within the community, as it is in many societies, this may be all that is considered. The prevalence of accusations within a household or between close kin, which may entail jealously concealing suspicions from the neighbours, may be largely ignored.

Other difficulties that made the broadest cultural comparisons unacceptable were amply demonstrated by the distortions produced by G.P. Murdoch's use of a statistical method to establish correlations between 'items' of culture in his Human Relations Area Files (he published, in 1957, a cross-cultural data set that consisted of 565 'cultures', coded for thirty variables). There were problems in determining the limits of 'a' culture; what was one distinct culture among several geographically and culturally related peoples? Other difficulties arose in classifying 'items' of culture that were to form the coded variables. For example, the label 'polygamous' might conceal considerable variation in marital arrangements, let alone ignore its social significance. Arguments over the definition of variables ensued. The statistical correlations that were produced could be misleading and disappointingly superficial. They might indicate some possibilities for comparison but they did not constitute satisfactory comparisons in themselves or lead to sound theoretical developments.

To point out the danger of misleading superficiality resulting from the attempt at universality is not a new claim. Where the analysis of witchcraft was concerned, it was the necessity for the inclusion of much ethnographic detail that made comparison cumbersome as it did with many other aspects of anthropological analysis. The anthropologists of the 1950s such as Schapera, Fortes, Richards and Nadel used regional comparisons to yield theoretical conclusions that might be tested elsewhere. Using such methods made it possible to set aside some of the common structural features of the societies under study to concentrate on the detail of similarities and differences in the aspect under consideration. This approach produced a wider regional interpretation that could then be set against similar general conclusions from other areas.[14] Nadel's work (1952) is particularly relevant here as he used this method to construct a theory of witchcraft comparing related and neighbouring peoples in the Sudan. His conclusion was that witchcraft was one of a number of alternative ways of explaining misfortune has become widely accepted, but his view that these alternatives were mutually exclusive was subsequently shown to be mistaken; beliefs in witchcraft may co-exist with beliefs in other causes of misfortune as I.M. Lewis showed (1970).

Ethnographic comparison as a method, whether between two societies or within a region, appears to be falling into disuse in recent anthropological works. However, this change does not mean that anthropologists no longer use comparative thinking. Anthropology is no more culture-free than science; its practitioners are all creatures of the cultures in which they were brought up. Implicit in their thinking there is always a framework of concepts and convictions that is derived from the thinker's own culture and that provides a comparison, unexamined and therefore uncontrolled. The distortion that is produced in this way has been labelled ethnocentricity, the bias that may distort anthropological analysis by an imposition of ideas that are not to be found in the material under review, but are derived from the anthropologist's own thinking. Julian Pitt-Rivers once remarked that the history of anthropology consists of a struggle to rid itself of ethnocentric thinking and he was probably right.[15] It is, of course, notoriously easier to detect this flaw in writings of the past and in one's colleagues' work than in one's own. However, making a comparison explicit and presenting evidence for one's conclusions are both essential as precautions and should never be ignored. This is particularly so where one of the societies in a comparison is one's own, as is the case in what follows.

Pocock suggested (1985: 43-44)[16] that it is necessary to consider the total context of a society's morality that structures understanding of the world and the people in it, rather than merely attempting to understand the meaning of its symbolic manifestations. All societies recognise a moral universe although it may not be formulated in terms of a binary distinction between good and evil as is the view derived from Christian ideas. With a comparative approach based on the underlying view of the world, parallels emerge that are not evident when the focus of the comparison is more narrowly defined. Thus the presence or absence of beliefs in witches and witchcraft is less important than the nature of the ideas represented in them. These chapters explore the similarities and differences between English[17] beliefs and those of some of the Africans living in London.

In the chapters that follow, the main comparisons use ethnographies of two aspects of modern England. The scale and diversity of the nation state presents serious problems, both of research and conceptualisation. Neither of the sets of beliefs that form the focus of my comparisons can be said to be universally held, as they are representative only of subsets of the population, although many of the ideas might well be shown to be more widely accepted when more research is undertaken. The first ethnography describes the movement concerning beliefs in a mythical satanic cult that were current at the end of the twentieth century;[18] and the second, accusations of witchcraft made against children, largely African in origin, which came to public notice in the very early twenty-first, although it is likely that cases which involved less violence had occurred before that time.[19] The former, as will be seen, reflects a long-lasting belief that is deeply embedded in English culture; the latter, though based on its own traditions, has emerged in its present form in recent years and results from the interaction of Christianity and the varied African beliefs in witchcraft. At first view the differences seem to have remained very striking, but these chapters attempt to reveal their similarities as well.

The next four chapters discuss the central ideas that reveal modern British beliefs in evil. The first of these focuses on the notion of hidden enemies of society – the fear of a secret conspiracy that aims to undermine the whole of social life. This fantasy as Cohn (1970: 3) pointed out, is flexible and can be directed at different groups of people at different times. As far as the twentieth-century belief in the prevalence of Satanism was concerned, its holders explicitly and publicly denied that they were Christian; if that were so, then their views showed that the ideas had become embedded in the whole culture rather being restricted to their source, the Christian Church. There have indeed been secular versions of this idea (Roberts 1974); there may also be a real enemy that is the source of the conspiracy, or equally the enemy may be imaginary.

In the original Christian formulation human sacrifice and cannibalism were believed to be practised by witches at the Witches' Sabbath, their

gathering to worship Satan. Chapter 3 suggests that contemporary killings, real or fantasised, may be wrongly interpreted as human sacrifices,
thus providing evidence of the alien nature of other societies. It discusses
the killings to procure human body parts for a form of powerful magic,
not referred to in the same terms as witchcraft or sacrifice, that has been
reported in Africa. These killings have frequently been referred to as
human sacrifices. By comparing them with the former use of human body
parts in European healing practices until the late eighteenth century and
in folk healing up until the nineteenth century, they can be seen for what
they really are. Occasional uses have been reported until the early twentieth century, and a contemporary form has been discovered recently in
Korea. Together with the preceding chapters, chapters 3 and 4 display the
differences between sacrifice, magic and witchcraft that cannot be properly understood when the label 'human sacrifice' is applied to them all
without careful ethnographic investigation and comparison.

None of these ideas of human physiology has survived without changes
and nor have ideas about human nature and behaviour. As chapters 6
and 7 show, the twentieth-century revival of new forms of fundamentalist
Christianity is spreading the ideas of original sin and the concept of evil
spirits owing allegiance to Satan as the cause of human evil in adults and
children. A major change in views about the nature of children and of
their displays of original sin has resulted in the adoption of extreme forms
of corporal punishment that, in the United States, have been declared
a form of child abuse (Heimlich 2011). Firth (1994), in his epigraph to
Hobsbawm's book on the twentieth century, remarks on 'the change from
a relatively rational and scientific view of things to a non-rational and less
scientific one', by which he means the revival of religious influence on
thought. The transformation of African ideas that has been achieved by
the missionary efforts of Pentecostal Christians is also described in chapters 6 and 7.

Chapter 8 analyses the dynamics that underlie the efforts of pastors of
independent African churches, created in the wake of the introduction of
Pentecostalism, to identify and exorcise the evil spirits that are believed
to cause witchcraft, particularly in children (Parkin 1985). Their aims are
ostensibly to fight evil and so purify society, but from the observer's point
of view their efforts seem to be a means of attracting a larger congregation and thus attaining personal success, which will be interpreted by the
laymen as God's support and approval of them.

The second half of the book thus highlights the changes that have taken
place in African beliefs in witches since the nineteenth century; the most
important is the introduction of the idea that children, even as toddlers
or babies, may be witches. This change comes from a fusion of Christian

and traditional beliefs and is discussed in Chapter 5 which is a rewritten version of one of the two in the collection that have already been published.[20] The subsequent chapters, 6 and 7, consider various aspects of these new beliefs and the way in which they are publicised and spread by the self-appointed pastors of charismatic African churches. Actual cases of children being accused of witchcraft are analysed in Chapter 8. In conclusion, the final chapter returns to the comparison between English and African forms of evil that retain their differences. The central claim of this chapter is that while beliefs in occult evil may vary in form from one society to another, the underlying ontologies allow comparisons to be drawn with each other and with Western beliefs, despite the varied spiritual entities which seem to offer different solutions to the problems of everyday human existence.

Notes

1 Durkheim was using the term to include the study of all society, so his use of it includes anthropology.

2 This type of research has been a defining characteristic of anthropology since the work of Malinowski in the Trobriand Islands during the First World War.

3 On two return visits, Lewis recorded changes in the villagers' views. See his final chapter, esp. pp. 244–51.

4 Evans-Pritchard made an implicit distinction between his attitudes to witchcraft and to religion later in his life when he made public his conviction that no one who had no religion could understand the religion of others. This view has not been generally accepted among anthropologists.

5 An early example is A. Macfarlane (1970).

6 The volume edited by Mary Douglas (1970) contains the papers presented at the conference.

7 Compare my, rather different, use of this comparison to understand the anti-satanist movement of the late twentieth century (La Fontaine 1998).

8 In later life Levy-Bruhl changed his views, apparently under the influence of Evans-Pritchard and other anthropological writing. In his notebooks published posthumously in 1949 he identified what he had termed 'primitive mentality' with creative thought and feeling, and called it 'something fundamental and indestructible in the nature of man' (cited in Tambiah 1981: 87).

9 'Superstition', as used today, denotes ideas and practices that are considered relics of earlier times or are thought to be irrational and untenable by most people; it is a distinctly derogatory label.

10 Although the activities of witch-hunters did cease, the beliefs, whether traditional or Christian, persisted. In England, for example, a woman was killed for alleged witchcraft as late as the nineteenth century. I owe this information to the research of James Nice, who kindly lent me his manuscript on *The Law and the Occult*.

11   In fact witchcraft beliefs have turned out to be just as lethal in the Third World as those that inspired the European witch-hunts. Independence has weakened the enforcement of colonial laws that made the killing of witches illegal, and post-colonial problems have encouraged the search for the human causes of distress.

12   The men and women who were known as 'wise' because of their occult knowledge might also be accused of witchcraft.

13   Gilbert Lewis (2000: 11–14) also points out the intermingling of cultural ideas with medical ones in concepts of illness.

14   Of these four, only Nadel was directly concerned with magic and witchcraft; the others wrote of political organisation or of kinship systems, but the methods were similar.

15   I have been unable to find a reference to this in his writings and think that he said it in conversation, perhaps in Chicago where we were both temporary members of the Anthropology Department at the university.

16   The citation is from the paperback edition 1986.

17   I use 'English' rather than the more usual 'British' because on this topic there are differences in the component parts of Great Britain and I have only done research in England. However I have noted that the cases involving allegations of Satanist activity in Scotland were very similar to those in England.

18   There is evidence that, as with the early modern witch-hunts, the beliefs are still held by former anti-satanists, though action on them is less frequent.

19   They continue to occur, although are largely ignored by the media.

20   One of these is Chapter 5, which is an updated version of my article entitled 'Child Witches' in *The Devil's Children : From Spirit Possession to Witchcraft, New Allegations that Affect Children* (2009). The other is Chapter 2, which is a slightly amended version of an article published in *Etnofoor*, republished by permission of the editors.

Bibliography

Ankarloo, B., and G. Henningsen. 1990. *Early Modern European Witchcraft: Centres and Peripheries*. Oxford: Oxford University Press.

Cohn, N. 1970. 'The Myth of Satan and his Human Servants', in Mary Douglas (ed.), *Witchcraft Confessions and Accusations*. London: Tavistock, pp. 3–16 .

Douglas, M. 1970. 'Introduction', in *Witchcraft Confessions and Accusations*, Association of Social Anthropologists Monographs 9. London: Tavistock, pp. xiii–xxxviii.

Durkheim, E. 1895. *Les Règles de la Méthode Sociologique*, trans. 1938 as *The Rules of Sociological Method*, ed. G. Catlin. Glencoe, IL: The Free Press.

Evans-Pritchard, E.E. 1937. *Witchcraft, Oracles and Magic among the Azande*. Oxford: Clarendon Press.

Favret-Saada, J. 1980. *Witchcraft in the Bocage*. Cambridge: Cambridge University Press.

Firth, R. 1994. 'The Century: A Bird's Eye View', in E. Hobsbawm, *Age of Extremes: The Short Twentieth Century 1914–1991*. London: Michael Joseph, p. 2.

Fortes, M. 1953. 'Analysis and Description in Social Anthropology', *The Advancement of Science* 10: 190–201.

Frazer, Sir J.G. (1890) 1922. *The Golden Bough*. London: Macmillan.

Goody, J. 1969. 'Comparative Sociology and the Decolonisation of the Social Sciences', in *Comparative Studies in Kinship*. London: Routledge & Kegan Paul, pp. 1–12.

Heimlich, J. 2011. *Breaking their Will: Shedding Light on Religious Maltreatment of Children*. Amherst, NY: Prometheus Books.

Henningsen, G. 1980. *The Witches' Advocate: Basque Witchcraft and the Spanish Inquisition 1609–1614*. Reno: University of Nevada Press.

Hobsbawm, E. 1994, pb. 1995. *The Age of Extremes: The Short Twentieth Century 1914–1991*. Michael Joseph and Abacus.

Kuhn, T.S. 1962. *The Structure of Scientific Revolutions*. Chicago: University of Chicago Press.

La Fontaine, J.S. 1998. *Speak of the Devil: Tales of Satanic Abuse in Contemporary England*. Cambridge: Cambridge University Press.

———. 2009. 'Child Witches in London: Changes in Religious Practice and Belief', in J.S. La Fontaine (ed.), *The Devil's Children: From Spirit Possession to Witchcraft, New Allegations that Affect Children*. Farnham: Ashgate, pp. 117–128.

Levi-Strauss, C. 1963. 'The Sorcerer and his Magic', in *Structural Anthropology*. New York: Basic Books, pp. 167–185 .

Levy-Bruhl, L. 1920. *Les Fonctions mentales dans les Sociétés inférieures*. Paris: Alcan.

———. 1949. *Les Carnets de Lucien Levy-Bruhl*. Paris: Presses Universitaires de France.

Lewis, G. 2000. *A Failure of Treatment*. Oxford Studies in Social and Cultural Anthropology. Oxford: Oxford University Press.

Lewis, I.M. 1970. 'A Structural Approach to Witchcraft and Spirit Possession', in M. Douglas (ed.), *Witchcraft Confessions and Accusations*. London: Tavistock.

Macfarlane, A. 1970. *Witchcraft in Tudor and Stuart England: A Regional and Comparative Study*. London: Routledge & Kegan Paul.

———. 1985, pb. 1989. 'The Root of All Evil' in D. Parkin (ed.), *The Anthropology of Evil*. Oxford: Basil Blackwell, pp. 57–76.

Middleton, J., and E. Winter (eds). 1963. *Witchcraft and Sorcery in East Africa*. London: Routledge & Kegan Paul.

Nadel, S.F. 1952. 'Witchcraft in Four African Societies: An Essay in Comparison', *American Anthropologist* 54(1): 18–29.

Niehaus, I. 2012. *Witchcraft and a Life in the New South Africa*. Cambridge: Cambridge University Press.

Parkin, D. (ed.). 1985. *The Anthropology of Evil*. Oxford: Basil Blackwell.

Peel, J.D.Y. 2015. *Christianity, Islam and Orisa-Religion: Three Traditions in Comparison and Interaction*. Berkeley: University of California Press.

Pocock, D. 1985. 'Unruly Evil', in D. Parkin (ed.), *The Anthropology of Evil*. Oxford: Blackwell, pp. 42–56.

Roberts, J.M. 1974. *The Mythology of the Secret Societies*. 2nd edn. St Albans: Paladin.

Tambiah, S.J. 1981. *Magic, Science, Religion and the Scope of Rationality*. The Lewis Henry Morgan Lectures. Cambridge: Cambridge University Press.

Thomas, K. 1970. 'The Relevance of Social Anthropology to the Historical Study of English Witchcraft', in Mary Douglas (ed.), *Witchcraft Confessions and Accusations*. London: Tavistock, pp. 47–80.

———. 1973. *Religion and the Decline of Magic*. London: Wiedenfeld & Nicholson.

Tylor, E.B. 1871. *Primitive Culture*. London: Murray.

Chapter 1

HIDDEN ENEMIES
Evil at the End of the Millennium

This chapter concerns the main framework of the Christian myth about witches: a conspiracy which is a Devil-worshipping cult that performs heinous acts of sexual abuse, murder and cannibalism in its rituals. Its revival at the end of the twentieth century instigated a moral panic about its victims, allegedly children and even babies. From the late 1980s until the mid-1990s, allegations that children had been sexually abused and even, in some cases, killed[1] in the course of rituals associated with Devil worship or Satanism were being made in Britain. To begin with, its members were referred to as witches but soon the preferred name for them was Satanists.[2] This label obviously derived from the identity of witches as the servants and worshippers of Satan, an element in the Christian myth that fuelled the early modern witch-hunt. In the modern version the organisation of Satanists was thought to have tentacles that stretched into every walk of life, so that its members were protected by policemen, judges, doctors and politicians. The failure to find and convict members of this secret conspiracy was taken as proof that powerful and exceedingly clever people were involved.

The allegations were very variable when looked at in detail. In many parts of Britain children were said to be telling of terrifying rituals in which they had been abused. Although labelled as cases of ritual or satanic abuse by those who reported them,[3] in some cases the evidence for doing so was rather slight. The commonest allegations concerned robed participants, pornography, sexual abuse and human sacrifice. There were usually several perpetrators (sometimes large numbers of them) allegedly involved, including women, and often several young children. Some highly publicised cases, in Nottingham, Manchester and the Orkney Islands were reported in the national press; others were less widely known but clearly part of the same phenomenon.

There was, from the outset, no independent proof of the existence of the satanic cults or of their activities, although in half the instances I collected there was evidence that children *had* been sexually abused. No reliable witnesses of the rituals came forward, although there were 'descriptions' by alleged victims. The police in various parts of England worked hard to find corroboration. In one case a child alleged that large, expensive cars had brought participants in the rituals to her house. Door-to-door canvassing by police failed to find a single person who had seen any Jaguars, Bentleys or Mercedes in their working-class London street. There was no evidence of murders having taken place either: 'no bodies, no bones, no blood, nothing'.[4] Believers saw this as the result of the demonic skill of the Satanists in concealing the evidence and of the power of their contacts, just as the absence of evidence for a conspiracy proved the power of conspirators.

What the evidence *might* have been, was demonstrated by the rare cases of sexual abuse that did involve rituals. There were only three. The perpetrators of the abuse claimed mystical powers to justify the abuse and also to frighten the children and one or two associated adults into silence. In these cases, and in no others, material evidence of what had happened was forthcoming: elements of altars, with cloths and garments that had been used, and books associated with the rituals were found by the police. This was evidence that supported the accusations made by the victims but in all three of them it was clear that the sexual motivation of the single perpetrator was primary and the ritual performance was secondary. I should stress that the evidence did not show any cult organisation. A lone perpetrator had initiated the acts leading to the abuse, although in two of the three cases they had recruited one or two other adults to participate in the rituals they had invented. Even in the one case where the perpetrator came to believe he was Lucifer, the illusion provided him with an excuse to abuse the children without ritual on many occasions as well. Finally there was no connection between the three abusers; each of them assembled a different cluster of supernatural ideas and practices, and the paraphernalia used in each case was unique to it. None of their ideas or practices resembled the ideas or actions of Satanism put forward by believers in the existence of the cults.[5] As far as satanic abuse went, these cases represented negative evidence.

The lack of independent corroboration was as true of America, Australia and continental Europe as it was of Britain.[6] The allegations were just that – allegations. The lack of independent support for them encouraged scepticism, but those who did not accept the allegations were left with the problem of understanding what was happening. The large number of cases and the way in which they appeared, spreading like a rash across Western countries, had been explained by those who believed in the theory of Satanism as evidence of an international conspiracy. For everyone else, the allegations of satanic abuse demanded explanations.

An obvious source of the ideas behind the fear of Satanism is fundamentalist and evangelical, particularly Pentecostal, Christianity.[7] Its publications include accounts by converts whose 'confessions' contrast the peace and beauty of the religious life with the evil and sinfulness, often represented as witchcraft and worship of the Devil, in their pasts. It is interesting to note how these accounts reflected current definitions of what acts were considered particularly evil.[8] In Doreen Irvine's book, *From Witchcraft to Christ* (1973), the witches who were the devil's disciples were involved in drugs and prostitution. But by the time Audrey Harper's *Dance with the Devil* was published in 1990, nearly twenty years later, sexual abuse and human sacrifice were integral to the ritual of the satanic cults she said she had joined.

While it is possible to trace a strong evangelical influence in the conferences, writings and videotapes produced by the campaigners against 'the Satanism scare', as it has been called, is not explicable solely as a Christian crusade. Many of the most vociferous in their allegations countered this claim by pointing to Jewish upbringings or atheistic convictions. Nor was it solely a popular means of raising a 'frisson'; accounts of satanic cases were reported in serious as well as sensationalist newspapers, and conferences were held in Britain and elsewhere at which experts, imported to start with from the United States, described the phenomenon to social workers, psychiatrists and policemen. There appeared to be a new and dreadful threat to children. The situation was serious enough for the government's Department of Health to fund research into what was happening.

The reliability of the allegations was powerfully supported by comparisons drawn with the established facts of child abuse. Immediately after the Second World War the new technique of X-ray had demonstrated that broken bones and skull fractures might not be accidental injuries. Although the passage of time did raise some doubts in particular cases, the public eventually accepted that children might be injured or even killed by those who should have been caring for them. Then came the revelation that incest was no myth and that children might be sexually abused by adults. The evidence for the sexual abuse of children was more debatable than the X-rays of broken bones that supported allegations of baby battering. Experts could and did argue about 'tests' for sexual abuse.[9] But to many, the new crime of sexual abuse was as well established as that for physical abuse. Ritual or satanic abuse, labelled in conformity with the earlier terms, seemed merely a further progression on the same path. Doubt was countered by pointing to the similar incredulity that had greeted the earlier revelations.

The ideas behind the notion of satanic abuse did not disseminate themselves merely through their own plausibility. They were actively

promoted by a variety of people, most of them with international connections in the movement, who were usually referred to as 'experts' on the
subject. Their approach was varied. Christians tended to take a mystical
approach, as can be seen in the view that the children taken into care
following allegations of satanic abuse should not be allowed to take any
objects from home, including favourite toys, since they or letters from
parents might be conduits of a satanic force that might be used to control
them. By contrast, the more secular experts seemed to have an approach
that derived more from the movements to promote belief in the stories
of abused children and the victims of rape. They clearly had influenced
much of the thinking of experts who came from the professional therapy
field.[10] The psychoanalytical axiom that what a patient says may be an
emotional rather than a factual 'truth', became transmuted, in the hands
of some of these 'experts', into the axiom that what such patients said
must be believed as fact.[11]

Where children were concerned, the claim was if anything stronger. The
assertion 'Children do not lie' became a dogma of the anti-Satanism movement, and 'Believe the children' a rallying cry.[12] These phrases recalled the
arguments advanced in favour of believing children who revealed that
they had been sexually abused. The strategy allowed campaigners against
satanic abuse to claim that their opponents wished to deny all mistreatment of children. On the other hand, children who did not recount a story
that might be made consistent with a diagnosis of satanic abuse were
believed to be repressing it, or to have dissociated themselves from traumatic memories. This view was popular in the United States, and trans-
mitted to the U.K. in conferences and in written form. Nevertheless most
evidence that was presented as what children had said was in fact the
result of adult selective recording and interpretation of their words (La
Fontaine 1997: Chapter 7).

In practice, children's evidence was less important than what the
experts provided as a way of diagnosing satanic abuse. Experts distributed lists of 'indicators' – symptoms that might indicate ritual abuse. They
were handed out at conferences and photocopied by those working in the
child protection services to distribute further. The indicators purported
to be derived from experience, and included many simple indications of
emotional disturbance (such as bed-wetting) as well as elements of more
bizarre behaviour. When distributed among social workers, foster parents and others who were struggling to understand the damaged children who had been taken into care, they facilitated the diagnosis of ritual/
satanic abuse as the origin of all disturbance. Crucially the lists bypassed
the necessity for children to make allegations, since the indicators were
deemed sufficient 'proof' of what had happened, and all that was then

required was to make children describe what the adults knew 'must' have happened.

A further proof of the existence of satanic abuse and a major cause of the outbreak consisted of adults, mostly women, who claimed to have suffered ritual abuse at the hands of satanic cults when children. What they said about their past would be claimed as an eye-witness account. Perhaps the most famous of these 'survivors', as they were called, was Michelle Smith. She was the co-author, with her therapist Lawrence Pazder whom she later married, of *Michelle Remembers*,[13] which was one of the sacred texts of the movement. Survivors' allegations were elicited by psychiatrists or counsellors (trained and untrained) and at least one article at an early stage pointed out the iatrogenic nature of the results (Mulhern 1991). A dramatic feature of the aftermath of the panic in the United States has been a series of court cases in which the survivors have sued their former therapists for the psychological damage done to themselves and their family relationships by the therapy.

Finally it is very important to remember the role of an element that is entirely modern and very influential: the media. Several journalists in England were keen supporters of the idea of satanic cults.[14] The flames were fanned by the competition between the various newspapers and television programmes. Some papers were sceptical but most appeared to express a firm belief in the allegations. But, as one sceptical journalist commented, 'Whichever way the story goes you get a good mix of weird sex, drug-taking orgies, bizarre regalia and ritual baby murder' (Anning 1991). The speed with which the scare spread doubtless owed not a little to the alacrity with which the media seized upon these attention-getting stories.

All these elements contributed to the nature of the scare and played a part in setting it in motion. However the factors that triggered one set of allegations in England do not provide a general explanation of similar sets elsewhere, let alone all such sets. For that we need to consider the phenomenon more analytically. The first accounts of the allegations – by Richardson, Best and Bromley (1991) in the United States, and by Jenkins (1992) in Britain – used the sociological theory of 'moral panics' as their framework to do this. The idea of a moral panic rests on the point of view known as social constructionist – that is, understanding social problems not as objective realities existing independently, but as the product of definitions of events made by interested parties and of their attempts made to persuade the public to adopt them. Cohen's definition, 'One can speak of a moral panic when the public reaction [as reflected in the media] is out of all proportion to the actual threat offered',[15] seems to fit the circumstances of the Satanism scare nicely when slightly modified to take account of today's press.

Those who study moral panics agree that the general state of society contributes the context in which definitions of problems are shaped, and there is also some agreement as to what factors are significant. The most often mentioned are serious and disturbing social change and economic upheavals, which create a general atmosphere of uncertainty. This was certainly true of the end of the twentieth century. The religious understanding of what might be expected at the end of the second millennium increased the general unease. Yet British society has suffered many periods of change and uncertainty since the end of the witch-hunts; why should it produce this scare now?

There is nothing in the theory of moral panics to specify how one identifies the precipitating factors rather than the more general predisposition in social conditions. In fact the books I referred to identified different antecedents. The first, about the United States, noted the rapid rise of fundamentalist Christianity, the anti-cult campaign which followed the spread of new religious movements, including many that were emphatically non-Christian, and the rise of the child protection movement. These elements provided the personnel and the ostensible reasons for the scare. Jenkins, writing about Britain, links the moral panic about satanic abuse to fears of a conspiracy of sexual predators and of threats to children. The social context he identifies as changes in the family, the influence of feminism, and the visibility of social problems because of the development of the mass media and the competition between newspapers. Jenkins further argues that the interdependence of panics is vital, and points to the essential links between a series of public panics in Britain about sexual abuse within the family, paedophile rings and the murder of children (Jenkins 1992: 14). He does not include the rise of evangelical Christianity as a major source of the scare, although he points out that 'the theories originated in fundamentalist circles' (ibid.: 17).

It is the difference between the two selections of antecedents that points to the weakness of the idea of moral panics in providing an explanation. The difference does not seem to be one of theoretical or analytical significance, but a matter of personal viewpoint. The theory (if it is one) does not specify the causes intermediate between the context – social change – and the panic itself. One must conclude that 'moral panic' is essentially a label,[16] useful as a means of identifying the phenomenon but not in explaining why it occurs.

There were differences in the Satanism scares between Britain and in the United States. In Britain those accused were mostly the parents of the alleged victims, together with unidentified Satanists; in the United States the accusations were most often levelled at the owners and staff of nursery schools by the parents of children who went there. This suggests the reflection of variable social anxieties that social anthropology has established may be mobilised in witch beliefs. However, the content of the allegations resembles those constituting accusations against witches worldwide. It is now a truism of anthropology (Parkin 1985) that almost all societies conceive of a figure representing the epitome of unregenerate evil, human but with more than human mystical powers, known usually in translation as 'a witch'.[17] All over the world, witches are shown as being 'not human' in their disregard of all the basic rules of human society: they are often said to commit incest or engage in cannibalism and vampirism for pleasure. Their inhuman status is symbolised in magical qualities that normal human beings do not possess (Pocock 1985). The Western allegations refer to hidden evildoers who resemble witches in their acts and in the mysterious powers they exercise.

Outbreaks of hunting witches outside Europe are discussed in the anthropological literature relatively rarely, although recent outbreaks have attracted attention.[18] These, however, show no close similarity to the recent Western scare. But if one turns to the past, witch-hunts in Western Europe and the United States of the early modern period do show striking similarities with features of the Satanism scare, both in the ideas of the witch-hunters and in the actions of the individuals and organisations involved. There is evidence of cultural continuity between early and late modern Europe.

To return to the past, the picture painted in the classic work by Norman Cohn (1975) was of a conceptualisation of evil that changed little in essentials over many centuries, but added details from time to time and place to place. The basic ideas – a secret cult performing rituals which involved sexual orgies, human sacrifice (often of children) and the drinking of blood – were present before the Christianisation of Europe, although it was the Church's linking of this image to the traditional picture of the witch that sparked off the witch-hunts. In the modern variant of the vision with which we are concerned, the orgiastic element includes the sexual abuse of children, who then become the victims of sacrifices. The twentieth-century conspirators were also believed to obtain access to sophisticated modern technology to obliterate evidence of their doings (one such was a portable crematorium run off a car battery). Looked at in this light, satanic abuse seems like the reappearance of a very old concept of evil in a modern version.

If this is so, we can make use of the ideas of historians as well as anthropologists to explain the Satanism scare.[19] Modern historians of the witch-hunts agree that it was the Church, determined to 'Christianise' the peasants and put an end to practices deemed 'pagan' or 'superstitious', that triggered the witch-hunts. The Church declared that witches obtained their evil power through a pact with the Devil, and portrayed them as worshipping Satan. The secular authorities supported the Church, their aim being to extend their control over outlying districts and centralise the power of the developing state. But the crusade against Satan and all his minions was a mission led by the Church, and many churchmen remained convinced of the existence of witches long after their pursuit had ended.

Witch-hunting came to an end when the authorities, both ecclesiastical and secular, withdrew their support for it. The witch-hunt did not just stop – it was stopped. An excellent example of this is spelled out in Henningsen's detailed account of an early seventeenth-century witch-hunt in north-eastern Spain (Henningsen 1980). The Jesuit, Alonso de Salazar Frias, sent by the Inquisition to investigate an outbreak of allegations of witchcraft there, became convinced that he was dealing with mass hysteria. His report, pointing to the lack of evidence in support of the allegations, was a triumph of rational argument and convinced the Inquisition, who ordered an end to the witch burnings.[20] The allegations soon came to an end.

The parallel with the modern situation seems, once again, very close. In England it was the involvement of governmental authorities, that is the social services and the police, that turned the stories circulating among fundamentalist Christians into a serious pursuit of a criminal organisation. Equally when the authorities, starting with the police, ceased to be convinced of its reality and the media stopped publicising cases, the momentum of the Satanism scare came to a halt. This is not to say that individual allegations did not continue, just as there were occasional pursuits of witches in England up until the end of the nineteenth century. From the seventeenth century to the end of the nineteenth there were occasional instances of attacks on people believed to be witches.[21] In Britain in 2004 there was a minor outbreak of allegations on the Isle of Lewis that was reported in the press some ten years after the end of the main satanic panic. Adult women, encouraged by their therapists and other supporters, continue to assert their status as survivors (that is as former victims) of satanic abuse.[22]

Cohn's account of *Europe's Inner Demons* is a story of continued development over time. In fact, belief in witches and evil spirits was not constant among the elite of Christian countries but rose and fell. In the eighth century St Boniface 'declare[d] roundly that to believe in witches and werewolves is unchristian' and Charlemagne announced that burning witches was pagan (cited in Trevor-Roper 1990: 13). Throughout the witch-hunts there seem to have been those who were sceptical and the recognition that the witch-hunts were profoundly mistaken rapidly took hold after the middle of the seventeenth century. By the middle of the twentieth century,

when I encountered them in Uganda, Christian missionaries were casti-
gating their converts for continuing to believe in witchcraft. Only pagans
and the superstitious believed in witchcraft, my African neighbours were
told. Yet by the end of that same century Christians in Europe believed
in the existence of Devil-worshipping cults, and some even referred to
them as covens of witches. The belief in witches seems to have waxed and
waned, rather than following a single course of development.

There are also reasons for caution in treating the satanic panic as a
resurgence of the ideas behind early modern Christian witch-hunts. The
belief in hidden conspiracies did not die when the hunt for witches ended.
It was kept alive in secular versions, particularly among the elite. J.M.
Roberts, writing of the myth of the secret societies, stated that, '[f]or about
a century and a half, large numbers of intelligent Europeans believed
that much of what was happening in the world around them happened
because secret societies planned it so' (Roberts 1974: 16).[23] Freemasons,
Jews, Communists and even the Boy Scouts were all, at one time or another
and by one person or another, considered to be surface manifestations of
a great international conspiracy, stretching across the civilised world and
seeking to undermine it.

The particular version of this myth that surfaced in the late twentieth
century as the panic about Satanism, was not the only panic of that time
in Britain, as Jenkins pointed out (Jenkins 1992). A scare about organised
paedophilia, which occurred at much the same time as the Satanism scare,
presented many of the same features: allegations of an organised conspiracy of men abusing children, where the lack of evidence was said to show
participation by the rich and powerful. They were alleged to be targeting
children's homes, and so police forces were set to combing the country
to collect evidence from former residents (see Webster 2005). In the end
only two out of the 365 children's home workers accused were convicted,
and they were not members of any conspiracy. Yet the rumours continued, and the lack of good evidence was said to be proof that the conspiracy reached into the higher ranks of the police, who were protecting the
guilty. The findings of the government inquiry into the matter appeared
to confirm the view that a hidden conspiracy was at work (Waterhouse
2000).

There is thus good reason to suppose that the myth of hidden enemies
has become part of British (and indeed Western) culture. It is not surprising that in the late twentieth century the discovery of the sexual abuse and
murder of children was assimilated to the myth and provoked a public
reaction. Satanic abuse is an image of evil acceptable to Christians and
non-Christians alike, and one that could be activated by individuals and
groups in pursuit of various aims.

I should make clear here that I am not arguing that the myth of hidden enemies is merely fantasy or collective paranoia. Everyday life provides material which may give the myth of the devil's disciples an appearance of incontrovertible fact. There are paedophiles and they sometimes associate with one another in gangs as recent trials have shown. Conspiracies and secret societies have actually existed, and some of them have aimed to overthrow the state, even if they did not worship the anti-Christ or seek to destroy civilisation. Towards the end of the nineteenth century many secret societies, like the Freemasons, did use occult symbols and conduct rituals of a definitely non-Christian sort. In more modern times the secular but secret IRA was seen by its Protestant opponents as satanic in inspiration, since it emerged from a Catholic/Papist community.

The mid twentieth century also saw the growth of many alternative religions such as the Unification Church of the Reverend Moon and the followings of other spiritual leaders. In addition there were groups modelling themselves on their concepts of pre-Christian religions; among them were those who called themselves Wiccans or witches. In the 1960s Anton LaVey founded an anti-Christian religion that he called the Church of Satan, and it gave rise to other self-styled Satanist groups. The beliefs of these new religions and their rapid success in converting people was profoundly threatening to the established religions, particularly to the growing evangelical wings of the Christian Church, which categorised them all as cults and claimed their practices to be evil and hence satanic.[24] It is not going too far to see the evangelical crusade against cultists as similar, although less violent, to the older church hunt for witches. Just as the sixteenth century witch-hunters could point to the curers and soothsayers in the villages as real witches, so the campaigners in the late twentieth century could say with truth that witches and Satanists actually existed. The allegation that they were engaging in extreme forms of paedophilia added modern forms of evil to the charges and, even more significantly, convinced the authorities of the need for action.

The essential foundation here is the increasing religiosity in social life. Despite their mutual hostility, the new Christian fundamentalism and the alternative religions share basic characteristics: both are founded on faith, on belief in the spiritual power to heal and change lives, either by performing ritual or channelling power through the charismatic leaders of the group, or both. Fundamentalism, whether Islamic or Christian, and the new religions all promote the idea that belief rather than logic or reason is the source of truth and the path to well-being. An extreme version of this view, as quoted by a well-known English novelist writing about multicultural Britain is: 'Unaided human reason is inferior in status to the gift of faith. Indeed reason is only useful insofar as it finds a use in the larger service of faith'.[25] Beside this militant assertion, the acceptance with which the conventional, more liberal versions of religion treat modern life seems defeatist.

This attitude has become increasingly common as fundamentalist forms of all world religions have become increasingly influential. More and more individuals have been recruited into groups that emphasise faith rather than reason. They may even regard the demand for verification not merely as an indication of scepticism and lack of faith, but as opposition, as a denial of faith that makes sceptics into enemies (Pocock 1985: 50–51) who must be defeated.

It is this change that underlies the Satanism scare and other panics. The connection with the past can be seen by looking at its inverse, the decline of witch-hunting in the seventeenth century. According to some historians, as Cartesian rationalism gradually became general in elite circles it led to a new scepticism that encouraged the authorities to stop the hunts (Trevor-Roper 1967: 122; Levack 1987).[26] Intellectual developments in the eighteenth and nineteenth centuries encouraged confidence in the power of reason to understand the world and in the ability of human intelligence to solve social and economic problems by accumulating knowledge. The decline of former modes of thought and the success of the scientific disciplines underlay ideas of progress; scientific knowledge of the world replaced the old biblical certainties. Rationality became the basis of intellectual life. Nineteenth-century anthropologists saw science as the highest stage of intellectual evolution that societies would eventually reach, replacing the traditional authority of religion.

By contrast, the late twentieth century could be said to show the loss of confidence in science and in arguments based on reason and logic. From being a part of general education, science has become a specialist and esoteric discipline, segregated from normal social life. It is no longer seen as an essential part of education and does not attract many, or necessarily the brightest, students. Hobsbawm (1995) has remarked that science has become identified with its technological products and they require no scientific understanding to operate. The harnessing of what is called 'scientific research' in the service of commerce adds to the disillusionment with science. The idea of continued progress based on scientific discoveries is a tarnished image. Science, and the technology that has followed its advances, has not solved the problems of the world; and some modern developments, such as genetic modifications and artificial aids to human reproduction, are suspected or even vigorously opposed by a hostile public. Scientific methods, such as the use of animals in experiments, are often attacked as unethical and those who use them declared to be morally repugnant.

Disenchantment with science has spread to other forms of the pursuit of knowledge. In the 1970s the notion that science was a means of explaining the world began to give way to the idea that there are numerous visions of reality, none better than any other. The post-modernist movement has taken this view even further. What is more, learning is no longer admired; Victoria Beckham, the famous footballer's wife, has recently declared she has never read a book in her life. Logic and reason retain their place in the universities but there is good evidence that the status of academics has declined sharply relative to other professions, as recent correspondence in the British press attests. Academics struggle to retain their autonomy in the face of increasingly dominating administrations. The universities appear to be regarded by the state as enterprises like any other, and the British government has encouraged commercial firms to take over the running of some schools, as though the profit motive provides the guarantee of a successful organisation.

The philosopher/sociologist Ernest Gellner (1992: 152) argued that the increasing esotericism of science has led to the intensification of the non-rational in other parts of social life. For him the development of psychoanalysis and psychiatry are prime examples of this trend. The religious renaissance is also evidence of a change of intellectual culture in the West. The claim that evolution is merely one theory among others exemplifies a direct challenge to rationality in its disregard of the nature of theories and of the tests that establish their validity. So too, moral panics are symptomatic of a mode of thought that is diametrically opposed to the rationality on which science and modern society have been built.

What these arguments have in common is their concern with the shift away from logic and reason that made it possible for the Satanism panic to develop. The existence of an idea of a threatening and secret conspiracy that has developed over the centuries as part of Western culture cannot explain why it produced a major international panic at the end of the first millennium. The social characteristics of that period of history that have been identified as favouring the spread of the Satanism scare were not confined to that time alone and therefore could not explain its rise either. But fundamentalism posed a challenge to what had become the conventional view of the world, a rational view favouring scientific explanation and reason. The spread of the Satanism scare was a demonstration of the strength of this challenge. Like the early modern witch-hunt, however, the pursuit of Satanists was stopped, and stopped largely through the use of rational enquiry. While I have followed a historical approach in arguing that British culture has a concept of evil that can break out in harmful moral panics about Devil worship, it is also clear that rationalism is still maintained, as Weber argued, as the basis of the bureaucracies that together form the structure of twenty-first-century Britain. Our demons and witches lie not far away.

Notes

This chapter was originally given as a lecture in the Saul Sidore lecture series at the University of New Hampshire, USA. I was honoured to be chosen to give the lecture and would like to thank everyone who made that brief visit there so interesting and pleasant. I have edited the lecture slightly as the original format was designed for an oral presentation, and it also needed updating.

1   The sacrificial victims were often babies. It was alleged that flaws in the process of reg-istering births would mean that some babies would have no public existence and were thus murdered with impunity.
2   The change was in large measure due to the efforts of neo-pagans to dissociate them-selves publicly from belief in the Devil, let alone worship of him. Modern witchcraft, known as Wicca or 'The Craft', is polytheistic and nature loving. The small number of actual Satanists in Britain denied practising sexual abuse or human sacrifice, but other-wise did little to protect themselves against such allegations.
3   To our postal survey of social services and police forces in England and Wales. See La Fontaine 1994.
4   This phrase, used by Rosie Waterhouse in an article for *The Independent*, became well known and widely used, especially among sceptics.
5   Nor did they resemble the rites of any new non-Christian religion or even that of a Satanist group such as the Church of Satan.
6   See Nathan and Snedeker 1995. In addition, a very much larger and more compre-hensive survey of ritual abuse allegations was carried out in the United States by a team of academics. Its conclusions were the same as my own. See Bottoms, Shaver and Goodman 1996.
7   Although, as Norman Cohn pointed out thirty years ago, the origin of the idea goes back before the Christianising of Europe. See his *Europe's Hidden Demons* (1975). My references will be to the Penguin edition 1976.
8   Amanda Sackur pointed this out to me, for which I am grateful.
9   Police and sexual abuse experts were at loggerheads on this issue in the famous cases in Cleveland in 1987.
10 Examples are Joan Coleman, a psychiatrist and the head of the Ritual Abuse Information Network and Support, and Valerie Sinason, now an analyst, who was reported recently as having said that she was still convinced of the reality of satanic abuse.
11 See Sinason 1994. Nevertheless, children's testimony was regularly reinterpreted by adults, and the distortions produced as evidence of ritual abuse.
12 'Believe the Children' was adopted as a title by an American organisation campaigning for recognition of the existence of satanic abuse.
13 Unusually, Michelle was a Catholic and was saved by her vision of the Virgin Mary, which ends the book. In addition, her husband had been a missionary in West Africa, and during his time there had heard of the traditional leopard societies and this clearly

influenced his thinking about cults. Both of these elements were untypical of the stories of survivors in general.

14 For example, Andrew Boyd, John Parker and Tim Tate, all of whom wrote books about the cult, although Tate's was withdrawn from publication at the last minute..

15 See Cohen 1972: 28 and Hall et al. 1978, cited in Jenkins 1992: 6–7 (my addition in square brackets).

16 Richardson, Bromley and Best would doubtless accept this, as they presented their book as a record of a new social phenomenon, not as an explanation of it, and they urged colleagues to undertake the necessary research to explain it.

17 There have been arguments against the use of this term as likely to bias enquiry, but as the concepts in different societies have so many features in common it is convenient to use a single term in comparing them. To distinguish the figure of evil from more mundane practitioners of black magic, the term 'night witch' may be used.

18 Some work was done in the past on witch-hunting in Central Africa in the 1930s – see Richards 1935; Willis 1968; Redmayne 1970. More recently the subject has been taken up again, but with a different approach (e.g. Comaroff and Comaroff 1993). Historians have made use of anthropological explanations but not always without provoking controversy within their profession. For criticisms of the approach see Thomas in Douglas (1970), Muchembled (1990) and Rowland (1990). The last two scholars contributed to the volume *Early Modern European Witchcraft*, edited by Ankerloo and Henningsen (1990).

19 Henningsen has also made use of this comparison (see Henningsen 1996).

20 As Henningsen points out, this did not end the trials but the spread of disbelief from a minority of officials in the Inquisition into society at large was very influential. Salazar's report is widely seen as the turning point in the history of the Spanish witch-hunt (Henningsen 1980: Preface).

21 I owe this information to the work on legal cases by James Nice, to whom I offer my thanks. Similarly, Henningsen (1980: 18) reports the murder of an alleged witch in northern France in 1976.

22 [22] In a seminar at the Child Protection Unit of the London Metropolitan Police directed by the former barrister Lee Moore, the existence of survivors was a key issue and belief in their veracity was insisted on.

23 [23] The quotation is from the second, paperback, edition.

24 For some fundamentalist Christians even other established religions, such as Islam, Hinduism and Buddhism, undertook Satan's work. The Pope was considered by some to be the anti-Christ himself, and the Roman Catholic religion a form of Devil worship.

25 Shabbir Ahktar, quoted by Hanif Kureishi in 'The Carnival of Culture', *The Guardian*, 4 August 2005.

26 My sketch is rather a crude one: there were individual sceptics in an earlier period just as some people remained believers in the Witches' Sabbath and the Demonic pact after the witch-hunts had ceased. I am referring here to the way of thinking of the majority.

Bibliography

Ankarloo, B., and G. Henningsen (eds). 1990. *Early Modern European Witchcraft: Centres and Peripheries*. Oxford: Clarendon Press.

Anning, N. 1991. 'How Satan Sold his Story to the Pops', *Journalist* (December/January): 5.

Bottoms, B., P. Shaver and G. Goodman. 1996. 'An Analysis of Ritualistic and Religion-Related Child Abuse Allegations', *Law and Human Behaviour* 20(1): 1–34 .

Boyd, A. 1991. *Blasphemous Rumours: Is Satanic Ritual Abuse Fact or Fantasy? An Investigation.* London: Fount Paperbacks.

Cohen, S. 1972. *Folk Devils and Moral Panics: The Creation of the Mods and Rockers.* Oxford: Blackwell.

Cohn, N. 1975. *Europe's Hidden Demons.* St Albans: Paladin.

Comaroff, J., and J. Comaroff (eds). 1993. *Modernity and its Malcontents: Ritual and Power in Postcolonial Africa.* Chicago: Chicago University Press.

Douglas, M. (ed.). 1970. *Witchcraft Accusations and Confessions.* London: Tavistock.

Gellner, E. 1992. *Reason and Culture: The Historical Role of Rationalism and Rationality.* Oxford: Blackwell.

Hall, S., et al. 1978. *Policing the Crime: Mugging the State and Law and Order.* London: Macmillan.

Harper, A., and H. Pugh. 1990. *Dance with the Devil.* Eastbourne: Kingsway.

Henningsen, G. 1980. *The Witches Advocate: Basque Witchcraft and the Spanish Inquistion 1609–1614.* Reno: University of Nevada Press.

———. 1996. 'The Child Witch Syndrome: Satanic Child Abuse of Today and Child Witch Trials of Yesterday', *The Journal of Forensic Psychiatry* 7(3): 581–593.

Hobsbawm, E. 1995. *The Age of Extremes: The Short Twentieth Century 1914–1991.* London: Michael Joseph.

Irvine, D. 1973. *From Witchcraft to Christ.* Cambridge: Concordia.

Jenkins, P. 1992. *Intimate Enemies: Moral Panics in Contemporary Britain.* New York: Aldine de Gruyter.

La Fontaine, J.S. 1990. *Child Sexual Abuse.* Cambridge: Polity Press.

———. 1994. *The Extent and Nature of Organised and Ritual Abuse: Research Findings.* London: HMSO.

———. 1997. *Speak of the Devil: Tales of Satanic Abuse in Contemporary England.* Cambridge: Cambridge University Press.

Levack, B.P. 1987. *The Witch Hunt in Early Modern Europe.* London and New York: Longman.

Muchembled, R. 1990. 'Satanic Myths and Cultural Reality in Early Modern Witchcraft', in B. Ankarloo and G. Henningsen (eds), *Early Modern European Witchcraft: Centres and Peripheries.* Oxford: Clarendon Press.

Mulhern, S. 1991. 'Satanism and Psychotherapy: A Rumour in Search of an Inquisition', in J. Richardson, J. Best and D. Bromley (eds), *The Satanism Scare.* New York: Aldine de Gruyter, pp. 145–174.

Nathan, D., and M. Snedeker. 1995. *Satan's Silence: Ritual Abuse and the Making of a Modern American Witch Hunt.* New York: Basic Books.

Nice, J. 'The Law and the Occult'. Unpublished manuscript.

Parker, J. 1993. *At the Heart of Darkness.* London: Sidgwick and Jackson.

Parkin, D. (ed.). 1985. *The Anthropology of Evil.* Oxford: Blackwell.

Pazder, L., and M. Smith. 1980. *Michelle Remembers.* New York: Pocket Books.

Pocock, D. 1985. 'Unruly Evil', in D. Parkin (ed.), *The Anthropology of Evil.* Oxford: Blackwell, pp. 42–56.

Redmayne, A. 1970. 'Chikanga: An African Diviner with an International Reputation', in M. Douglas (ed.), *Witchcraft Accusations and Confessions.* London: Tavistock, pp. 103–128.

Richards, A.I. 1935. 'A Modern Movement of Witchfinders', *Africa* 8(4): 448–461.

Richardson, J., J. Best and D. Bromley (eds). 1991. *The Satanism Scare.* New York: Aldine de Gruyter.

Roberts, J.M. 1974. *The Mythology of the Secret Societies*. 2nd edn. St Albans: Paladin.

Rowland, R. 1990. '"Fantasticall and Devilishe Person": European Witch-Beliefs in Comparative Perspective', in B. Ankarloo and G. Henningsen (eds), *Early Modern European Witchcraft: Centres and Peripheries*. Oxford: Clarendon Press.

Sinason, V. (ed.). 1994. *Treating Survivors of Satanic Abuse*. London and New York: Routledge.

Trevor-Roper, H.R. (1967) 1990. *The European Witch-craze of the Sixteenth and Seventeenth Centuries*. Harmondsworth: Penguin Books.

Waterhouse, Sir R. 2000. 'Lost in Care'. Report of the North Wales Tribunal of Inquiry into Child Abuse. HMSO.

Webster, R. 2005. *The Secret of Bryn Estyn: The Making of a Modern Witch-hunt*. Oxford: Orwell Press.

Willis, R. 1968. 'Kamcape: An Anti-Sorcery Movement in South West Tanzania', *Africa* 38(1): 129–140.

Chapter 2

Concepts of Evil, Witchcraft and the Sexual Abuse of Children in Modern England

'Evil', as David Parkin remarks in his introduction to a collection of essays on the *Anthropology of Evil* (1985), is not an easy tool for anthropologists to use in cross-cultural comparison. To define one's terms is essential if readers are to be clear about what is the focus of attention. In this chapter I follow a suggestion made by one of the contributors to Parkin's volume who concentrates on human action, its moral evaluation and use as a means of drawing a line between the human and the inhuman, or evil. Pocock (1985) argues, with reference to contemporary English society, with which I am also concerned, that certain actions are considered evil, whether the term is used or not. This human behaviour is seen as contrary to, and destructive of, all order. Those who commit these acts are seen as having placed themselves outside normal society or even humanity as a whole. Hence evil is what is inexplicable in normal human terms. Pocock argues, as against Macfarlane's view that in modern England the term is obsolete (Macfarlane 1985: 57), that any reluctance to use it is not because it embodies ideas that are no longer held, but because it is too strong. He bases his remarks on informal investigations, both literary and conversational (Pocock 1985: 49). For the majority of individuals, and particularly for Christians, certain acts do indeed characterise the actors as 'evil'. Pocock points out that to attempt to explain evil 'was regarded [by the majority of his informants] at best as misguided and at worst as participating in the very evil that, by explaining, it appeared to extenuate' (ibid.: 51). What is condemned as inhuman cannot be explained. Pocock claims, however, that a minority of people exist for whom 'faith in the human capacity to explain is absolute' (ibid.: 50). For them, the label evil must be withheld because, if all the circumstances of human action are known, explanation is always possible. In effect, the refusal of the minority to use the term 'evil' confirms that they share with the majority a sense of the term's reference to the inexplicable and inhuman. This is why they do not use it.

Evil, then, according to this view, is implicit in those acts which are beyond the limits of explicable behaviour, and so emphasise the boundaries between the human and inhuman. Pocock does not consider the acts themselves; the one act he does mention as incurring condemnation as evil is a sexual assault on a child. Paedophilia has long been regarded with horror in Britain, despite a tiny minority of persons who argue that children may consent to sexual activities and should be permitted to experience them. The idea of incest did not provoke such deep feeling, largely because, as I have argued elsewhere (La Fontaine 1990: 26–27), its association with forbidden marriages and with reproduction implied sexual activity between adults. As a result the idea of incest was separated from the concept of sexual activities with children. It was the idea of strangers kidnapping, sexually assaulting or even killing children that evoked the sort of reaction that incest provokes in other societies. The recently demonstrated fact that children may be sexually abused in their own homes is not easily accepted and may still be vigorously denied; this is because it negates the fundamental assumption of parental altruism that underpins the concept of the family. Insofar as the public has accepted the reality of incest as involving children being sexually abused, the perpetrators are regarded as 'beasts' and 'monsters' and are so characterised in the popular press. Among convicted criminals, who transgress many of the legal and moral norms of society, those convicted of sexual crimes and particularly sexual crimes against children, are execrated. Significantly, 'beasts' is the slang term for them (Pocock 1985: 56). They are usually segregated in prison for their own protection (La Fontaine 1990: 21).[1]

The sexual or physical abuse of children, particularly very young children, serves in modern England to exemplify a major form of evil and to characterise those who commit these acts as inhuman monsters. Yet a minority continue to look for a way of rendering this behaviour explicable and so transforming the unintelligible into something which can be understood and, it is implied, prevented. During my research into the sexual abuse of children I was often asked why people do such things. The implication, it was clear, was that if abusers were human beings then human motives could be found for their actions. Yet any explanations I advanced mostly failed to satisfy the questioners, because they seemed incommensurate with the enormity of the offences. Sexual assaults on children could not be seen as other than something to be totally repudiated, and the idea that adult human beings could engage in sexual activity with children was seen as 'not normal'. One explanation that might be advanced instead was that the people concerned were mentally ill, hence excluded in a different way from 'normal' humanity. Other epithets that carried the same connotations were 'inhuman', 'animal', and, on several occasions, 'really evil'. Those who used them usually rejected altogether the possibility of explanation.

There are other acts that provoke similar reactions. Since the Slaughter of the Innocents by Herod, killing children has been an example of human evil in Christian societies. Parents who batter their children are considered as monstrous as those who sexually abuse them. Stories that troops were bayoneting babies circulated on both sides during the Second World War and shocking stories of children's sufferings are still used as examples of evil, whether attributed to particular individuals or displayed as the results of disasters. During the Gulf War, reports that Iraqi troops disconnected incubators in a Kuwaiti hospital, leaving new-born infants to die, were used to emphasise the inhumanity of Saddam Hussein's regime and justify calling him an 'evil man'. Human sacrifice and cannibalism are other examples of what the majority of English people would consider 'savage', the practices of people who are scarcely human. Sexual perversions, killing and torture, particularly of the young and harmless, cannibalism and human sacrifice are all enactments of evil in European eyes. An article in *The Guardian* confirmed this association. Making the point that extreme behaviour is now to be found depicted in easily available videos, the authors remark that 'sadomasochism, serial murder cannibalism are all on general release ... Democracy has made evil as accessible as air travel' (Cohen and Taylor 1992).

It could still be argued that there is no modern English concept of an evil that is distinct from acts that are condemned as such. Both Pocock and Macfarlane use beliefs in witchcraft as they existed in the European past and in other cultures to point up by contrast the character of the English beliefs they are discussing. In most of the societies that anthropologists have traditionally studied, inhuman evil is personified in the mythical figure of the witch. The term 'witch' is the accepted translation of words in indigenous languages that refer to a cluster of similar, but not identical, ideas. They have in common reference to acts that are perceived as transgressing the fundamental moral axioms on which human nature and hence society is based, and serve as the epitome of evil (La Fontaine 1963: 214; Parkin 1985: 1). Witches are human in form, yet lack intelligible human motives, while displaying the propensity to commit evil for its own sake. Their inhuman natures are exhibited in extra-human attributes, such as the ability to fly or to leave their bodies apparently sleeping while they travel on their nocturnal business. Their modes of attack, referred to in English as 'witchcraft' or 'sorcery',[2] demonstrate powers that are manifestly not human: human organs are thought to be removed without visible signs, leaving the victim to sicken and die. Witches may cause harm to a human being or animal merely by speaking of, or looking at, it; even their malicious thoughts can be the cause of illness or death. The attribution of apparently ridiculous or trivial qualities to witches serves to underline even further their intrinsically inhuman nature. As Pocock puts it, 'they symbolise what human beings *are* not, and not only what they *should* not do' (1985: 48).

If we consider the acts that are thought to be characteristic of witches, they show a remarkable consistency across cultures. Sexual depravity, often epitomised as incest but including bestiality and all socially forbidden forms of sexuality, is one of them. Murder, even of one's own children, and cannibalism are others. The killing of kin who normally have the strongest claims to protection is, like incest, the denial of kinship, the most basic of all relationships. Killing others out of what Hume called 'disinterested malice',[3] or to indulge in eating human flesh, are, like perverse sexual appetites, attributes of the apparently human creature who is beyond the moral pale.[4] The attribution of such sins to witches may vary in their detail and emphasis according to the cultural issues, but they commonly concern breaking fundamental social assumptions about what is natural human behaviour in relation to sex, food and mortal violence. In modern England, evil inheres in very similar acts: in the sexual abuse, ill-treatment and murder of children, in cannibalism and human sacrifice.

Nevertheless the forms in which similar concepts of evil are represented are strikingly different. English 'beasts' and 'monsters' have no mystical powers attributed to them; the perpetrators of evil are human beings, whereas witches are not just inhuman but possess supernatural powers. In modern English thought, evil consists in the behaviour of human beings, even though, once detected, they reveal the author of the actions to be a monster in human form. The allegations concern material rather than mystical damage. Modern evil lies in causing pain and suffering by physical means. Child battering can be demonstrated by Xrays and medical evidence. In many cases of the sexual abuse of children there is medical evidence to show that children have been physically injured. Pocock concludes: '[I]n primitive societies evil is attributed ultimately to monsters that cannot exist, whereas in our society it is attributed to monsters that do' (1985: 56).

There is a further difference between beliefs in witchcraft and these anthropocentric concepts of evil. Witches are not merely powerful and autonomous symbols of evil; witchcraft is also held to be the cause of a wide range of lesser misfortunes and suffering. Normal human beings may be thought to resort to witchcraft or sorcery on occasion for the understandable, though not morally defensible, reasons of envy, jealousy or spite. Human malice is neither generalised nor unprovoked although it may cause harm in ways similar to those used by witches. Misfortune of all sorts may be laid at the door of these human witches, but the human use of witchcraft is distinguished from the persistent evil-doing of witches. Accusations of witchcraft can therefore be made against human beings without necessarily branding them as embodiments of all evil and of committing the more terrible of the stereotypical witch's acts. In some societies, people may even accept a reputation for using witchcraft as a protection from attack by others; they would be careful not to allow people to believe they were witches. Nevertheless, if the incidence of unfortunate events is thought to be the 'proof' of the presence of witchcraft, that presence is also a reminder of the existence of inhuman but invisible witches of the more deadly kind. Witches, witchcraft and human suffering are linked conceptually in a triangle of evil to which there appears to be no counterpart in modern English concepts.

In the past, European witch beliefs seem to have resembled those documented in other parts of the world more closely.. Magic was practised by 'cunning folk' who used charms to heal human beings and animals, to protect against witchcraft, *maleficium* and to identify thieves or witches. The cunning folk might also be accused of using their mystical powers to harm rather than help, as magicians in Africa might be. Folk belief in witchcraft concerned the harm done to neighbours, by the occasional practice of witchcraft: to damage property, harm livestock or cause sickness, especially to children. Accusations were made from time to time against those with whom the sufferer had quarrelled recently. Historians have emphasised that, at least in England, popular belief did not link witches with the Devil (Macfarlane 1970: 189; Thomas 1970: 49–50; Cohn 1975: 251–53[5]) and was little concerned with witches as opposed to the manifest effect of the witches' craft.

A stereotype of evil that appears to have been current more among the literate than the peasantry, but which became more widespread during the witch-hunts of the sixteenth and seventeenth centuries, has also been documented. Cohn demonstrates the extreme antiquity of a cluster of ideas that linked the idea of secret organisations with rituals performed at night that included the killing of babies, cannibalism and sexual orgies of shocking depravity. Its origin predates Christianity and the ideas appear to be deep-seated in European culture rather than associated with any particular group or religion. Cohn dates the first allegations to the second century AD when accusations were made against the Christians, culminating in episodes of dreadful persecution and killings in Lyons at the end of the century. Even then, in promoting fears of a secret and evil conspiracy,

the allegations drew on earlier myths of conspirators sealing their com-
pacts with each other by a cannibalistic feast and on accusations of holding licentious orgies made against the followers of Bacchus by a Roman
consul and reported by Livy (Cohn 1975: 10). It came to be widely thought
that Christians practised ritual murder and cannibalism and that they
indulged in promiscuity, even involving their children.

The establishment of Christianity as the religion of Europe turned the
allegations back against the enemies of Christianity. Ritual murder, cannibalism and sexual debauchery came to be seen as inspired by Satan
and his demons. Magic, sorcery and consorting with demons were considered to represent a survival of paganism, and was later associated
with heretical beliefs deemed hostile to the Church. Over the following
centuries the myth developed, adding elements to the original form but
not changing its essentials: 'Again and again, over a period of many centuries, heretical sects were accused of holding promiscuous and incestuous orgies in the dark; of killing infants and devouring their remains; of
worshipping the devil' (Cohn 1975: 54). Demonic beasts, and in particular
the cat and the goat (both symbols in Europe of promiscuous and exces-
sive mating) became associated with the Devil, as his incarnation or as
the familiars of witches. With the charges fabricated by Philip of France
against the Templars, homosexuality and sodomy were added to the list
of the depravities of Satan's followers. The blood libel against Jews –
secret rites in which babies were sacrificed – presents the murder of babies
as human sacrifices, a horrifying rite comparable to cannibalism (Dundes
1991). The characteristic features of these beliefs in extreme evil – secret
rites, murder, cannibalism and unimaginable sexual depravity – persisted
relatively unchanged until their mobilisation in the great witch-hunts of
the early modern period.

This stereotype of evil appears not to have been closely connected
to the actions of real people except when it was mobilised against the
current enemies of the Church. It was not until the period of the great
witch-hunts that folk beliefs were attacked and the stereotype of evil was
linked with *maleficium* and the magic of the peasants. By the beginning
of the period when the great witch-hunts took place, witches had been
declared by the Church to have a contract with the Devil, and the evil
powers they possessed to have been provided by him (Cohn 1975: 100).
During the great witch-hunts, the pamphlets of the witch-hunters and the
confessions extracted under duress or even torture added details to this
picture. Witches were believed to be organised in covens, to fly at night
to their meeting places on monstrous animals or even implements such
as brooms, which were anointed with secret ointments made with the fat
of sacrificed babies. The covens celebrated 'sabbats', a term taken from

the Jewish religion which was generally believed to be the prototype of 'apostasy', the denial of Christianity. The proceedings included the worshippers formally renouncing the Christian religion, worshipping Satan and offering him gifts. It was at this point in history that Satan came to be depicted as half man, half monstrous goat, of terrifying appearance. Wild dances and orgies in which all normal controls on sexuality were relaxed, were part of these nocturnal celebrations.

It has been pointed out (Cohn 1975: 12; Macfarlane 1985: 59) that the more elaborate ideas of witchcraft and Satanism were to be found in canonical writings, in the anti-witchcraft pamphlets and writings of fanatical witch-hunters, and in the confessions extracted by the Inquisition under torture. It was the canonical view and the myth of a satanic conspiracy, according to Cohn (1975: 252–53), that precipitated the witch-hunts rather than the fears of the people in the possibility of *maleficium* or mystical evil. Macfarlane alleges that a general and more widespread belief in a satanic conspiracy distinguished continental Europe from Protestant England. Nevertheless, even in England, there were to be found beliefs that resembled those current in the rest of Europe. In one such case in Essex, the unusual features were explained by the presence of witch-finders who, it was suggested, would know of the canonical views (Macfarlane 1970: 6, 139). During the witch-hunts, given the tensions among villagers and the influence of the Church and educated people generally, villagers accused of witchcraft were easily prevailed upon to confess to the more exotic practices. Accounts of previous confessions were widely circulated, and gave witch-finders and examiners of the accused ideas of what to look for. The successful detection of witches and their execution in large numbers must also have reinforced local belief in the allegation that there was a widespread conspiracy threatening society. The link between mythical evil and those suspected of using witchcraft against their enemies in the community was thus reinforced.

It is commonly thought that the ancient beliefs in magic, sorcery and witches have disappeared, either as a result of the spread of ideas of rational explanation under the influence of science or because of the social changes that have taken place since the end of the great witch-hunts. Macfarlane (1985) argues that confidence in man's control of the world and the relativity of judgements in a society in which money mediated all relations has banished beliefs in the immanence of evil in the world, and hence, by implication, beliefs in witchcraft. Medicine, the Church and the Law took over from the cunning folk their roles as diagnosticians of, and purveyors of remedies for, illnesses and misfortune (Thomas 1970). Pocock, while arguing that concepts of evil are not obsolete among the majority, describes the rationalist minority as though they reflect the same intellectual change that Macfarlane claims has affected the whole society (Pocock 1985: 50). Understanding based on the rational foundations of industrial society appears inimical to concepts of mystical evil as a force in everyday life.

It is characteristic of beliefs in witchcraft that malice is directed as a spiritual attack or is magically activated in sorcery. The occasional malice of (still) human beings is, it is true, no longer implicated in suffering or misfortune. The link between misfortune, the ill wishes of enemies and evil has apparently been severed by the development of rational explanations for these events. Yet the existence of disbelief at different times and places, among people of differing religions and cultures, should make us wary of associating scepticism about mystical evil with modern, 'scientific' thought. There were sceptics at the earliest times; Cohn records that before the fifteenth century the educated had rejected folk witch beliefs (1975: 224). Even at the height of the witch-hunts of the sixteenth and seventeenth centuries, there were individuals whose scepticism has been preserved in records. The early Christian Church, as has been indicated, saw beliefs in witches or demons as inconsistent with true faith; believers in magic were guilty of denying the omnipotence of the Christian God. The view that beliefs in magic and witchcraft were essentially pagan superstitions that must be eradicated was still taught by Christian priests in Uganda during the 1950s.[6]

There is other evidence that casts doubt on the vulnerability of beliefs in evil, whether of the occasional, human, kind or more terrifyingly associated with unseen beings, to the spread of 'scientific' knowledge. Studies of the effect of European culture and technology on beliefs in witchcraft in colonial Africa have indicated that they are very resistant, even to radical changes in social life and in culture. Some anthropologists have concluded that the response to change was a greater, rather than lesser, fear of witches and a manifest eagerness to accept new means to combat them (Douglas 1970: xix–xxii).[7] The appearance of new and radical movements against witches, described as witch-finding cults, in Central Africa during the colonial period was interpreted as a response to the fears of populations who attributed the radical upheaval in their social lives to witchcraft. In eastern Uganda in the 1950s, church membership was seen by some as offering the same sort of protection. Anthropologists have accepted, since Evans-Pritchard's work on the Azande (1937), that witchcraft beliefs form an explanatory system, but it has been too often assumed that more effective forms of explanation, such as are provided by 'science' and rationalist approaches, will supersede them. Yet Evans-Pritchard demonstrated clearly that beliefs in witchcraft are to be understood, not as an alternative to more 'rational' or 'scientific' explanation, but as a form of theodicy expressing an apprehension of evil, both human and inhuman. Since social change does not eradicate the problem of understanding suffering or misfortune, the forms are not discarded, but only altered to fit new social circumstances.

Proof of the survival of the ancient European forms in which evil is conceptualised has been forthcoming in recent years. The more gross forms of the sexual abuse of children have come to be associated with all the other forms of evil in allegations of organised evil. An account by the social worker who led the team dealing with a case in Nottingham stated: '[W]e realised that these children had been born into a world where good had to be destroyed, innocence perverted. It was difficult to hear properly at first – difficult to grasp how evil people could be' (Dawson 1990: 13). This case, it was asserted, differed from other cases of sexual abuse, in the degree of damage to the children and in the events surrounding the abuse. The Nottingham case, although not the first, has become the touchstone of all subsequent cases and has been followed by a number of others in which similar allegations have been made. The events surrounding the sexual abuse of children are described as rituals directed to the worship of Satan or as witchcraft; the term 'ritual (or satanic) abuse' has been coined to describe them. They differ from other cases of children who have been sexually abused in that the circumstances of the abuse are said to include sexual orgies, animal and human sacrifice, and, in some cases, acts of cannibalism. Television and radio programmes, national, local and weekly newspapers have all carried dramatic stories linking the sexual abuse of children to witchcraft, 'the occult' and Satanism. Some initial claims were supported by a Member of Parliament, Geoffrey Dickens.[8] In 1989, a television programme, The Cook Report, implied that an occult bookshop in Leeds was encouraging Satanism in Britain. Broader allegations of an international network of satanic cults amounting to a worldwide satanic conspiracy, appeared in *Deliverance*, a book by the Christian Deliverance Study Group, and were quoted in *The Times* (Gledhill 1990). Our survey,[9] designed to discover the incidence of cases in which allegations have been made, resulted in sixty-two reports of alleged ritual abuse occurring over a four-year period between the beginning of 1988 and the end of 1991. These cases form a minute proportion of the total incidence of the sexual abuse of children, but they have received a disproportionate amount of publicity.

Broadly speaking, the accounts of ritual abuse resemble what has been called the canonical or satanic view of witchcraft, rather than the folk model. There is no evidence that beliefs resembling those of the ideas of villagers in Tudor and Stuart Essex have contributed anything to modern English beliefs in Satanism. There is, however, a close parallel between the content of modern allegations and the nature of accusations made against heretics, witches and Jews at various periods of history. As well as making general allegations against certain categories of people, there are also specific accusations against those either charged with the children's sexual abuse or alleged to be its perpetrators.

One difference between these cases and the charges made against witches in former times lies in the apparent absence of mystical powers attributed to the members of the cult. They are described as human beings engaged in the worship of evil. Yet the ability of the participants to avoid identification does add an element of mysterious power to their nefarious doings. The successful evasion of detection is not given mystical explanations: it is attributed to superior intelligence, threats of harm or death made to deter informers, or the presence in the group of powerful individuals who can protect the others from investigation and/or prosecution (Boyd 1991: 164–67).The impression given is that the people concerned are powerful as well as evil; incidents reported included: pets found dead with their bodies drained of blood, strange intrusions into the house with no visible sign of entry, threatening telephone calls to unlisted numbers, and being followed by mysterious means to addresses no one was supposed to know. Some social workers have even asked for police protection. Accounts of mysterious threats delivered to those who listen to the victims of ritual abuse circulate freely (Boyd 1991: 89–92; Core and Harrison 1991: 148–50). The fear they inspire resembles the fear of supernatural beings in that they imply an invisible danger against which it is impossible to protect oneself.

The difference between late twentieth-century beliefs in evil and those from other societies lies, I would argue, not so much in the content of the beliefs but in the fact that they exist in competition with others, diametrically opposed to them. Witchcraft accusations in African societies involve political conflicts (Middleton 1960; Turner 1954), but these take place within a moral system in which the beliefs are widely accepted; it is only the validity of particular accusations that may be denied. In contemporary British society it is the existence of this form of evil itself that is in dispute. The concepts of evil are politically embedded in a different way. A sketch of the opposing groups may serve to demonstrate this more clearly.

Although the belief in the existence of Satanists, Devil worshippers and witches is seen as Christian in origin, those who believe in the reality of ritual abuse vary in their religious affiliations; some do not describe themselves as Christians. While Christian believers may accept that Satan himself may be present in the ritual, many others accept it as an act of worship in an alien and evil religion. The existence of this religion or a national or international conspiracy is also not inevitably accepted by those who believe that ritual abuse is happening. They may argue that the trappings of Satanism or witchcraft are included, either for the perverse pleasure of the adult participants or to intimidate the children and prevent them telling anyone of their sexual abuse. For the purposes of this chapter I shall refer to all these people as 'believers', although it should be emphasised that their beliefs are by no means uniform. They have in common only the conviction that the ritual abuse has happened as described. However, even those who profess themselves to be atheist as far as their religious convictions are concerned are inclined to attribute evil to those who hold beliefs that can be described as 'witchcraft' or 'satanism', or who show interest in what is loosely described as 'the occult'.

Scepticism in the late twentieth century is more widespread and vocal than it seems to have been in earlier times. The accounts of ritual abuse have been vigorously challenged and extensively criticized. In opposition to those who proclaim them as true, sceptics have pointed out the lack of supporting evidence in the cases in which ritual abuse has been alleged, to prove that the rituals ever took place. They have underlined the failure of police investigations to discover forensic evidence of meetings or of killings, whether human or animal, and emphasised the vagueness of descriptions and the unreliability of the witnesses. Some of the sceptics argue that the 'rituals' are merely appurtenances of the sexual abuse of children and indeed of adult victims, to be understood as manifestations of sexual perversion. They argue that there has been no demonstration of the beliefs which would make such behaviour ritual in any other than a psychopathological sense. Others have gone further and cast doubt on the existence of any cases of sexual abuse of children, whether or not in ritual circumstances. The spread of concern about ritual/satanic abuse has been described as a 'moral panic' and various groups of evangelical Christians have been accused of encouraging the stories in order to further their missionary activities and/or to prove the approach of the end of the world. In some of the more extreme forms, the sceptics' view of evangelical Christians seems to imply a wicked conspiracy, though a different one from that believed in by their opponents. While the believers claim to be fighting the evil that will destroy society, the sceptics label its existence a delusion.

The situation is complicated by the existence of a third, rather heterogeneous, category of people who can be labelled occultists: people whose very varied religious beliefs and practices are based on interest in the occult and who belong to new, that is to say recently established, religions (Adler 1986, Barker 1989; Luhrmann 1989). In many ways their position resembles that of the heretics against whom accusations of Satanism were made, and the parallel may be made explicit in identifications of both as Devil worshippers. Since the 1950s, the spread of interest in occult systems of thought and in the creation of new religions has resulted in the establishment of small groups of occult practitioners, some of whom describe themselves as witches (or, more properly 'Wiccans' as they call their religion Wicca; see Hutton 1999) or Satanists. The majority of Satanists (La Fontaine 1999) belong to two 'churches' of Satan, founded in the United States; they are a small minority among occultists, who are themselves a small minority in the British population. Some believers associate interest in the occult with ritual abuse and seem to see all occultists as at least potential abusers of children; others have learned to distinguish between Wiccan groups and others. The occultists claim that they have suffered prejudice and even attacks by those who assume that it is their members who perpetrate ritual abuse. They are angry at being falsely accused and nervous lest lack of understanding of their activities may turn into wholescale persecution, like the witch-hunts of early modern Europe. Unlike sceptics or rationalists, occultists do not deny the possibility of mystical evil, but assert categorically that they do not use it. The claim, that some of them make, that no practitioner of modern Wicca or Satanism is ever guilty of abusing a child flies in the face of research, which makes it clear that no category of persons can claim to be above suspicion. Apologists for modern Satanism usually gloss over the encouragement of self-indulgence, violence and sexual extremism in their credo that might well attract disturbed people to the groups. In the general ignorance of what occultism is, the occultists' use of terms such as magic and witchcraft for their practices makes it easy for believers to identify them with the perpetrators of ritual abuse.

Believers and occultists resemble each other in that both may use a view of the past to validate their positions. Believers point to what they see as a similarity between modern accounts of ritual abuse, the historical accusations of witchcraft as practised in early modern Europe and the practices of modern witches and Satanists (Tate 1991: 58–103; Boyd 1991: 108–20). They argue that this proves the persistence of Satanism since the beginning of Christian times. Occultists may quote Margaret Murray (1921) and, sometimes, Sir James Frazer (1922), to support their claim that witchcraft is the survival of a pre-Christian religion that has suffered periodic persecution by illiberal Christians. Believers ignore the fact that their sources for early modern witchcraft and its connection with Satan worship are such writings as the *Malleus Maleficorum*, a manual for Inquisitors, and Christian allegations against heretics such as the Cathars or self-interested denunciations such as those against the Templars (Cohn 1975: 75–98). The occultists' claim to the antiquity of their religion is also based on spurious evidence (ibid.: 99–146) and ignores the other victims of the accusation of evil conspiracy, including Christians themselves. Both appeal to different versions of historical myth, with scant regard for historical accuracy or evidence. Much of the thinking of both groups is based on dogmatic assumption and arguments that do not bear rational scrutiny. Both believe in powers of good and evil, although they differ radically as to where they are to be found.

The ranks of the sceptics are augmented by those who are concerned, less with the sexual abuse of children, than with the protection of traditional society from what they see as attacks on it. Intervention by the state in what is seen as the 'private' domain of the family is evidence of such attempts to undermine a 'traditional way of life'. Attacks on social workers are popular among the working class who fear them, and the conservatives who resent what is seen as state interference. In particular there is a wish among some people to deny that children are ever sexually abused within their own homes. In such views, the allegations against parents are false and the people who make them evil because they seek to attack a fundamental institution, the family, and hence to destroy the very fabric of social life. The diagnosis of sexual abuse in what seemed like a large number of children in Cleveland in north-east England in 1988 caused a major public controversy which became a fierce political contest (Campbell 1989; La Fontaine 1990: 1–13). The report of the Judicial Inquiry (Butler-Sloss 1988) which followed did not pronounce on the truth or otherwise of the allegations and, as a result, failed to satisfy some people on both sides of the debate or defuse the feelings it evoked. The affair and its aftermath can be understood as evidence that what was at issue in the public at large was not simply a practical concern about what happened in Cleveland, but also a debate about the legitimacy of state intervention between parents and children. Since to a large number of people parental care is assumed to be both natural and altruistic, to accuse parents of inhuman acts like sexual abuse was not merely a malicious lie, but evidence of a dangerous conspiracy to undermine the family.

The association of the sexual abuse of children with the existence of an evil conspiracy raises moral issues with which many shades of opinion can be associated. Identifying the different components of the opposing constituencies in the Cleveland affair showed how such broad issues mobilise differing and even contradictory views under a single banner. The use of fundamental issues of morality as a means to transform individual beliefs into commitment to a public campaign may reflect the scale and heterogeneity of the society in which the moral struggle takes place. In small-scale societies, accusations of evil mobilise the factions within small local groups, activating ties of kinship, affinity and neighbourhood in a community that shares common assumptions. In a larger political arena, particularly one in which there is no homogeneity of belief, waging a campaign against the evil within takes a different form. The particular form I am concerned with, and its persistence over many centuries, suggests that this is no recent development but a characteristic feature of Western society. The nationalism of the nineteenth and twentieth centuries has tended to obscure the fact that the reality of European polities has long been that of a kaleidoscope of different languages, religions and local cultures. In such societies the moral basis for authority is located in no single source of legitimacy and is vulnerable to challenge.

In England today, the question of whether children are being abused in satanic rituals is not simply a matter of differing personal opinions, but also one of public controversy, raising questions of practical policy and law enforcement. Large amounts of public money have been spent on judicial inquiries and police investigations, and the time of many public employees, such as child protection workers, has been taken up with the cases and their aftermath. The question of belief in the reality of ritual abuse is now a political contest, in which both sides attempt to gain public legitimacy and popular support. The ultimate goal is to influence action by the state. To consider such concepts simply as ideas, without setting them in the social context of action, would have distorted the object of my enquiry. The account in this chapter has aimed to show that evil is more than a social construct – not merely an abstract notion but an idea with important consequences in social action.

Notes

Paper given to the Anthropology Department at the University of Amsterdam, published in *Etnofoor* V(1), February 1992. I thank the department for the invitation to discuss my ideas at the start of research on this topic, and *Etnofoor*'s current editor for permission to republish this paper. This version has been edited slightly and brought up to date.

1   This protection is necessary. In a riot in Strangeways Prison, Manchester, in April 1990, a wing where such prisoners were segregated was attacked; one man, who had not yet been tried for an accusation of sexually abusing a child, subsequently died of his injuries.

2   Evans-Pritchard proposed a distinction between sorcery – 'the use of black magic', and witchcraft – 'the infliction of harm by mystical means'. His definitions were used extensively by his students but became more controversial as ethnographic knowledge accumulated. See Turner 1954. Here I use the English 'witch' to include sorcerers and black magicians as embodiments of evil.

3   Referred to in Pocock (1985: 44, 47).

4   In some societies both human sacrifice and cannibalism have been practised (see Chapter 5) but in those societies the circumstances in which such acts might be possible or even required were clearly specified. They were never acts that an individual might indulge in at will. Witches' feasts in Africa were not acts of worship, but feasts. They consumed the spirit of the human flesh, not its reality, causing weakness and disease in the individual whose body was spiritually 'eaten'. European witches were believed to eat the bodies of those they had sacrificed to Satan in a reversal of the Christian ritual.

5   All page references are to the 1976 Paladin edition.

6   During my fieldwork in Uganda I heard a long sermon preached in Bugisu by an African Protestant priest, in which he inveighed against those un-Christian villagers who persisted in attributing misfortune and suffering to human malice rather than divine punishment. He concluded by characterising such people as evil and, in doing so, referred to them by the Gisu term that I have translated 'witch' (La Fontaine 1963: 192).

7   Movements to eradicate all witches that broke out in central and eastern Africa during the early colonial period resembled in many ways the movements against heretics or witches in Europe, except that they did not have the approval or support of the authorities. On the contrary they were banned and firmly suppressed.

8   See also his introduction to Harper 1990.

9   My research into organised and ritual abuse was funded by the Department of Health; for the survey I collaborated with the Department of Social Work and Social Policy of Manchester University. Their project, directed by Bernard Gallagher, was funded by the Economic and Social Research Council. The paper on which this chapter is based was written before the research was complete.

Bibliography

Adler M. 1986. *Drawing Down the Moon*. Boston: Beacon.

Barker, E. 1989. *New Religious Movements: A Practical Introduction*. London: HMSO.

Boyd, A. 1991. *Blasphemous Rumours: Is Satanic Ritual Abuse Fact or Fantasy. An Investigation*. London: Fount Paperbacks.

Butler-Sloss, Lord Justice E. 1988. *The Report on the Cleveland Affair 1987*. London: HMSO.

Campbell, B. 1989. *Unofficial Secrets: Child Sexual Abuse – the Cleveland Case*. London: Virago.

Cohen, S., and L. Taylor. 1992. 'Have We Got to Get Out of this Place?', *The Guardian*, 25 August.

Cohn, N. 1975. *Europe's Inner Demons*. Sussex: Sussex University Press, in association with Heinemann Educational Books. Paperback Edition 1976, Paladin: St Albans, Herts.

Core, D., and F. Harrison. 1991. *Chasing Satan*. London: Gunter Books.

Dawson, J. 1990. 'Vortex of Evil', *New Statesman/Society* 3 (5 October): 12–14.

Douglas, M. (ed.). 1970. *Witchcraft: Confessions and Accusations*. ASA Monographs No. 9. London: Tavistock.

Dundes, A. (ed.). 1991. *The Blood Libel: A Casebook in Anti-Semitic Folklore*. Madison: University of Wisconsin Press.

Evans-Pritchard, E.E. 1937. *Witchcraft, Oracles and Magic among the Azande*. Oxford: Oxford University Press.

Frazer, Sir J.G. 1922. *The Golden Bough*. Abridged edition. London: Macmillan.

Gledhill, R. 1990. *The Times*, 9, 7 November.

Harper, A., with H. Pugh. 1990. *Dance with the Devil*. Eastbourne: Kingsway.

Hutton, R. 1999. 'Modern Pagan Witchcraft', in *Witchcraft and Magic in Europe; Volume 6. The Twetieth Century*. London: Athlone Press.

La Fontaine, J.S. 1963. 'Witchcraft in Bugisu', in J. Middleton and E. Winter (eds), *Witchcraft and Sorcery in East Africa*. London: Routledge & Kegan Paul, pp. 187–220.

———. 1990. *Child Sexual Abuse*. Oxford: Polity.

———. 1999. 'Satanism and Satanic Mythology' in *Witchcraft and Magic in Europe; Volume 6. The Twentieth Century*. London: Athlone Press.

Luhrmann, T. 1989. *Persuasions of the Witch's Craft*. Oxford: Basil Blackwell.

Macfarlane, A. 1970. *Witchcraft in Tudor and Stuart England*. London: Routledge & Kegan Paul.

———. 1985. 'The Root of all Evil', in D. Parkin (ed.), *The Anthropology of Evil*. Oxford: Blackwell, pp. 57–76.

Middleton, J. 1960. *Lugbara Religion: Ritual and Authority among an East African People*. London: Routledge & Kegan Paul.

Middleton, J., and E. Winter (eds). 1963. *Witchcraft and Sorcery in East Africa*. London: Routledge & Kegan Paul.

Murray, M. 1921. *The Witch Cult in Western Europe*. Oxford: Oxford University Press.

Parkin, D. 1985. 'Introduction', in D. Parkin (ed.), *The Anthropology of Evil*. Oxford: Blackwell, pp. 1–25.

Pocock, D. 1985. 'Unruly Evil', in D. Parkin (ed.), *The Anthropology of Evil*. Oxford: Blackwell, pp. 42–56.

Tate, T. 1991. *Children for the Devil: Ritual Abuse and Satanic Crime*. Unpublished.

Thomas, K. 1970 *The Relevance of Social Anthropology to the Historical Study of English Witchcraft*', in M. Douglas (ed.), *Witchcraft: Confessions and Accusations*. ASA Monographs No. 9. London: Tavistock, pp. 47–80.

Turner, V.W. 1954 *Schism and Continuity in an African Society: A Study of Ndembu Village Life*. Manchester: Manchester University Press.

———. 1964. 'Witchcraft and Sorcery: Taxonomy versus Dynamics', *Africa* 34(4): 314–25.

Chapter 3

RITUAL MURDER?

Ritual murder was a term much used in the late 1980s and early 1990s to describe one of the activities of unknown groups of people who were believed to be worshipping Satan in ceremonies composed of the most evil acts. The significance of these ideas formed the subject of the last chapter. In the public mind, ritual is religious action; the solemn acts of Christians, Muslims, Hindus and others in which they worship their gods in designated forms of worship. It is public, solemn and holy as befits communication with a spiritual power that, in the case of Christians, is understood as the Creator of all things. Ritual concerns the sacred and it is a truism of anthropology that the sacred also constitutes the greatest legitimacy that can turn power into authority. Ritual is sacred action.

Murder is, by contrast, immoral and illegal; it is an act carried out, often in secret, that attracts a severe penalty. In all societies killing human beings is subject to some form of conceptualisation (see Bohannan 1960: 230–35), that defines which killings are culpable and which are not. Unlawful killing is murder. In Western (i.e. Christian) doctrine, any killing of a human being is wrong: Thou shalt not kill' is one of the Ten Commandments. This is the moral position; but in law not all killings have the same status. Some killings are not considered murder; they may be classed as homicides, either culpable or not, as accidents, or undertaken as punishments (see Smith 2000). In other societies there may also be exceptions to a general rule but not necessarily the same ones. Some of these exceptions may designate categories of human beings who are virtually rendered non-human and killing them breaks no moral rule. In eastern Uganda, sorcerers and homosexuals were excluded in this way; killing them was not 'murder' and entailed no blood guilt. This attitude, common in Uganda generally, has not changed but rather intensified; there is a currently a proposal to make homosexuality punishable in law – by death. In many societies, killing, whether allowable or not, may be believed to pollute the murderer who must be ritually cleansed; the victim's kin may incur a duty to seek vengeance or compensation. Murder, then, is the prototype of illegitimate action, the opposite of a religious act. Ritual murder is thus a contradiction in terms, an oxymoron that demands explanation.

In Europe ritual murder epitomises the worship of Satan, the god of evil and during the early modern period it was believed that the central act of the Witches' Sabbath was the sacrifice of human beings, particularly babies, to Satan. The bodies were then consumed in a communal feast. Elements of this centuries-old myth were clearly to be seen in the allegations of the Satan hunters at the end of the twentieth century (La Fontaine 1998, 1999).

Ritual murder is a link to the realm of spiritual powers, but those of great evil. It is thus symbolically appropriate that it combines the most holy with the most evil. Human sacrifices during rituals have been observed and documented in the past, and these may be referred to as ritual murder by outsiders; but the label can also refer to a much more shadowy concept, invoked often enough to describe imagined atrocities or to denigrate particular communities, but never substantiated by reliable evidence or observations (see Kahaner 1994). In fact, ritual murder remains a Western idea representing all that is evil, which denotes the alien nature of people outside what may be known as 'the civilised world'. It may, as we have seen in previous chapters, be associated with the horror of the evil within one's own society. As an inhuman evil it has much in common with witchcraft.

The impetus to write this chapter was given by a film in the television series, *Dispatches*. It concerned a number of killings in Uganda that were referred to both as ritual murder and as human sacrifice. The labels were wrongly applied and the programme was misleading, so various anthropologists, myself included, challenged the film-makers. Journalists are often considered to be more sceptical than most people but in this case they could be said to accurately represent the culture of the society they came from. The film was deeply ethnocentric, an excellent example of what the French historian Muchembled wrote of the analysis of ideas that fails to consider their social context. He pointed out the likelihood that 'the investigator will describe his own mental processes rather than the subject of his research' (Muchembled 1990: 141). This could have been avoided if the film-makers had used either some anthropological expertise or at least the comparable material that had already been made public.

The focus of the film and the cause of this major disagreement between film-makers and anthropologists was the alleged rapid increase in frequency, in Uganda, of murders, particularly of children, who were killed and then mutilated. These cases were referred to as 'child sacrifices' or ritual murders. In support of their view the film-makers relied heavily on a man who 'confessed' to having killed seventy individuals, but to have reformed. He claimed to be mounting a campaign against child sacrifice in expiation. Most of the anthropologists did not believe this, recognising the type of Christian leader whose conversion gains added lustre from the contrast with the blackness of former sin. In addition, anthropologists spend much time evaluating what they are told and checking one person's account against another's; they rarely accept a single account without back-up from other evidence. While the film-makers reported that they had been told by reliable witnesses of multiple killings and mutilations, a Ugandan anthropologist from Makerere referred to the subject of the film as 'hysteria', and linked it to the popularity of Nigerian ('Nollywood') films in which such killings feature.[1]

Professor Pat Caplan (2010) wrote an article about this controversy for *Anthropology Today* which provides a useful summary of the film and its aftermath. Her aim was not to decide on the rights or wrongs of either position but to discuss the main topics she thought had been raised by the controversy, one of which is relevant here. The first concerned 'the interpretation of witchcraft and other forms of alleged ritual killings in contemporary Africa', while the second, which I shall not consider, had to do with the media and what she called 'public anthropology'. She argued that anthropologists are inclined to interpret allegations of witchcraft as ideas and moral values in the classical tradition, implying that this leads them to deny the reality of such beliefs. Whether by reality is meant that some people actually are witches or that what they do actually works is not made clear. Caplan points out that, in an alternative view of 'occult phenomena', 'some anthropologists working in Africa have accepted that there has indeed been an increase in allegations of witchcraft, but also *in its material manifestations, including killing and the removal of body parts*' (my italics). Here killing for body parts is identified with witchcraft; the other material manifestations are not specified. It is not common to find anthropologists identifying murder for body parts as witchcraft as it is clear that the severed body parts were used in magical concoctions. However, there are anthropologists who argue that making distinctions between magic, witchcraft and sorcery is not helpful. My view is that, on the contrary, there are important distinguishing features. The most important is that magic is a technical act that can be performed on behalf of someone else; witchcraft is the result of the witch's *own* malice directed against its victims.

I turn now to what we know about killings that are linked with beliefs in occult phenomena in order to find an appropriate and helpful comparison, and I start with human sacrifice.

Human Sacrifice

The killing of a living creature as a ritual offering to a god or spirit used to be termed a 'blood sacrifice', an old-fashioned term that focuses attention on the spilling of blood. The blood may be important, less in itself than as a manifestation of the despatch of a victim's life as an offering to the spiritual being or beings to whom the ritual is addressed. Usually a return is expected in the form of good fortune, whether generalised or as the granting of a particular prayer. Blood sacrifice might also be used to cleanse sufferers from sin, to prevent misfortune or failure, or to avert evil. In some places and times the blood spilled was human.

However, not all sacrifices entail the spilling of blood; victims were killed in other ways, and in some societies and on some occasions it was actually important not to spill the victim's blood (see Evans-Pritchard on Nuer sacrifice). The reference to blood has now been dropped for good reason, since the spilling of blood is not diagnostic of sacrifice, and explains little about it (see van Baaren 1964). Instead anthropologists may discuss sacrifice without necessarily distinguishing forms of it (and see Smith and Doniger 1989). Sacrifice is a part of rituals in many parts of the world, although usually the offering takes the form of an animal or even a bird. The more valued the creature sacrificed, the greater the honour done to the recipient of the offering.[2] Most anthropologists in the field in Africa have seen at least one of these sacrifices, usually involving a chicken or a goat.

The most valuable life of all is that of a human being, and so human sacrifice, where it occurred, was the greatest possible ritual gift. Human sacrifice has been recorded in many parts of the world although, as historians have pointed out, executions and other killings of human beings have sometimes been wrongly interpreted as human sacrifice (Wilks cited in Law 1985). The most famous example of it is perhaps that of the Aztecs, whose human sacrifice allegedly consisted of a heart taken from a living victim.

There is evidence that human sacrifice took place in societies, including some in what is now Britain, that bordered on the Greek and Roman empires, whose sacrifices were restricted to animals and birds. Some authorities attest to the practice of child sacrifice in what is now the Middle East. Abraham's acceptance of God's demand that he sacrifice his only son was sufficient as an offering, so Isaac was not killed, but Jephthah's daughter died willingly as her father's offering. Archaeological remains of the burials of babies that had been killed seem to provide good evidence that child sacrifice in this area was not a myth but an actuality.

Rituals including human sacrifice have also been described by outside observers. In Central America the practice of human sacrifice among the

Aztecs and Incas was recorded by the invading Spaniards in early modern times, and in parts of Africa by the Europeans who came first as traders and then as missionaries and colonisers. There is most information on human sacrifice in Africa, where it was first recorded by Arab travellers as far back as the tenth century. It was described in more detail by later European visitors to West Africa, who went both as travellers and as professionals, as employees of the new colonial powers. I will draw largely on that material as summarised in a very useful article by the historian Robin Law (1985). There is no doubt that this killing took place as part of public rituals and was considered legitimate.

In Africa by the nineteenth century, human sacrifice, which had been more widespread, was a practice largely confined to some kingdoms of West Africa, such as Asante, Benin, Dahomey, Calabar and the riverine Ibo, although a general disregard for human life was much more widespread.[3] Where sacrifice still continued, human beings were killed as offerings to gods and to the dead, particularly dead kings and other elite forebears. In the West African kingdom of Dahomey, a regular ritual of remembrance offered to dead kings, known as the Annual Customs, required the sacrifice of human victims to strengthen the dead rulers' spiritual powers and, by showing filial piety, engage the royal dead on behalf of their successor. It also demonstrated the mundane power of the ruler and the legitimacy of his position (Law 1985). The former function was explicitly recognised by one such ruler, King Kpengla of Dahomey, who explained succinctly the need for human sacrifice to a European enquirer in the 1780s as follows: 'You have seen me kill many men at the Customs. This gives a grandeur to my Customs, far beyond the display of fine things which I buy. This makes my enemies fear me and gives me a name in the bush' (Olfert Dapper, cited in Law 1985: 74).

In West Africa, as in ancient China and elsewhere, funerals might entail the killing of human beings to accompany the dead. A great ruler might be buried with his wives and/or members of his entourage to provide him with a suitable retinue in the afterlife. The individuals who were killed were not, strictly speaking, sacrificed, since they were not killed as offerings either to the gods or the spirit of the dead king or ruler. Moreover it is alleged in some cases that the close associates of the dead man volunteered to die, much as Indian widows were traditionally expected to commit suicide on the funeral pyre of their dead husband.[4] Nevertheless, the term 'human sacrifice' may be used to refer to these practices, since the additional deaths were an integral part of the funeral ritual. In parts of West Africa, individuals might also be killed as messengers to the dead in addition to the normal human sacrifices. Fear of the approaching colonial powers resulted in many human sacrifices to avert military disaster.

Killings as offerings to the dead may not seem to Westerners to be sacrifices, in that they are not offerings to gods. However, as is well documented in ethnography in many African religions, ancestors are holy beings, with spiritual powers to reward or punish their descendants. There may be some recognition of a vaguely conceptualised creator god but as a remote deity, uninterested in human affairs; the ancestors are usually the spirits to whom one appeals for help in trouble. Thus in Dahomey, when human sacrifices were made 'to water the graves of the ancestors', they were as much a part of their religion as other religious festivals. Hence we may call these sacrifices, and where the victim was human they were human sacrifices.

Two patterns among the selection of victims can be seen. The victim for sacrifice may be chosen either as a particularly pure or valuable human being: a child, a virgin or a young warrior; alternatively the opposite choice may be made, with the victim being an outsider: a captive, a representative of a defeated enemy, or a slave. Slaves might also be bought to be sacrificed, thus avoiding the need to kill a member of the community. However, where the tally of captives and slaves was insufficient, victims might be taken by force from among members of local communities.

Both the Greeks and the Romans offered blood sacrifices to their gods but they were never human sacrifices, although they did keep slaves whom they might have sacrificed. In fact the Romans characterised some societies on the margins of their empires as 'barbarians', specifically because they did perform human sacrifices. The failure to draw a distinction between human beings and animals, which the existence of human sacrifice implied, was to both Greeks and Romans clear evidence of the lack of civilisation of those people who practised it. Those they conquered, such as the tribes in what is now Britain, were strongly discouraged from the practice. In the early centuries of the Christian Era from which this information comes there were increasing number of Christians within the Roman Empire who believed that the death of Jesus was 'a full, perfect and sufficient sacrifice for the sins of the whole world' (The Book of Common Prayer 1928), and it rendered any sacrifice not merely unnecessary, but a failure of faith. Pagans who offered sacrifices to their gods were seen as barbarians. Thus sacrifice and, in particular, what was sacrificed, was a powerful symbol for both Christian and non-Christian communities, dividing them and justifying to each the inferiority of the other.

Human sacrifice is no longer practised, even in those societies where it used to be part of the traditional religious rites. Apart from the disapproval of the Romans, the spread of Christianity in territories taken as colonies by European powers, starting with Spain and Portugal in South America in early modern times, have rendered it immoral and illegal in many areas where it used to be practised. Islam, spreading down from North Africa to south of the Sahara, put an end to the practice in the north of many West African states and further colonisation by the European powers in the nineteenth century forcibly ended the practice in the southern areas.[5] There may be talk of its revival in independent West African states where it has only been a century or so since the practice was stopped, but the stories are, so far, only unconfirmed rumours. There has been no public return to the practice, but Westerners persist in associating Africa with human sacrifice (see also Schmidt (2009) on a similar association with Haitian *vodun*). Since the practice is abhorred in Britain it may also be seen as (ritual) murder.

There are also practices that are sometimes confused with human sacrifice or considered to be necessarily linked to it. Cannibalism is not an inevitable consequence of human sacrifice nor are the victims dismembered for use in some other way, although the Aztecs were reputed to eat the hearts of human sacrifices. Some peoples, in many different parts of the world – the Ijo of West Africa are an example – ate parts of their dead enemies as a means of magically taking over their strength (Law 1985: 58).[6] Marshall Sahlins describes with some gusto similar practices in Fiji (2003). Such practices have been referred to as 'ritual cannibalism', since they have magical and spiritual connotations for the participants. However, in Africa, although animal sacrifices were normally eaten at the end of a ritual, in a feast whose participants were carefully selected for their relation to the spirit (usually an ancestor) in whose honour the sacrifice had been offered, human sacrifices were not often eaten, nor were the bodies dismembered. Speaking generally, cannibalism, even as a ritual, was always much less frequent than human sacrifice (Law 1985: 58).

The rationale for eating human sacrificial victims, or enemies who had been killed in battle, was that power was thought to be inherent in parts of the human body, even after death; eating them incorporated it in the eater's body.[7] The same belief lies behind the more modern use in Africa of body parts in 'medicines'[8] (see the next chapter for a fuller discussion). These 'medicines' are concoctions whose purposes are purely secular and individual; they are put together by 'specialists', who charge for their services, for the purpose of enhancing their clients' health, wealth or success in life. The use of human body parts is said to give the magic very great power.

The individuals who specialise in this form of magic, often referred to as witchdoctors, may employ killers to obtain what they need or may kill themselves.[9] In both cases the killing is secret and entails no ritual; the subsequent magical substance is concocted in secret by the magician who then hands it over to his client in exchange for a large payment. The recipes for such 'medicines' are not revealed. Universally stigmatised as 'bad' or 'evil', the practice has nevertheless been reported in widely separated areas of Africa.

The 'child sacrifices' in Uganda were almost certainly killings for such magical purposes. The police reported that some corpses lacked limbs or organs. Murders for body parts are not offerings to any god or spirit but killings for gain: both the client who orders the 'medicine' and the magician/sorcerer who prepares it aim to profit by the death. While the belief in the power of human body parts may be called magical thinking, as can the idea that albino body parts have greater power than normal African ones, the killing is not part of any ritual. Children and young people may be chosen as victims more often because of their purity and the potential for growth in their bodies, but their selection may simply be the more mundane one of greater ease of capture. We do not know, as everything about these 'medicine' killings is secret until the mutilated body is found. Whereas human sacrifice was performed openly and as part of rituals that were believed to benefit the community, these murders are furtive and hidden, fuelled by individual ambition and the lust for wealth and power. They are manifestations of a continuing belief in the power of magic or sorcery, but not of witchcraft, which has never rested on material proof except for the misfortunes that are, with hindsight, attributed to it. Killings for '*muti*' (a Zulu term, which will be explained further in the next chapter) are openly condemned by members of the communities where they take place, but they are not human sacrifices or even ritual murders.

Ritual Murder

If ritual murder is not human sacrifice or killing to obtain ingredients for powerful magic, what is it? The term implies a killing to obtain spiritual powers that are not recognised as morally right, but are evil and dangerous. So far from being the same as human sacrifice, ritual murder is its antithesis.

It is in Western Europe that one finds this idea of ritual murder, and it has a long history. In the second century AD, Christians may have despised the religion of their pagan neighbours for the blood spilt in their rituals, but much worse allegations were made against these small dissident groups within the Roman community (see Cohn 1975; Rives 1995). Christians were said to worship their god in secret, performing rites in which there were sexual, often incestuous, orgies and cannibal feasts. This seems to have been the earliest linking of these three acts as denoting extreme evil.[10] The central act of the ritual was said to be the killing and eating of a child or baby, perhaps stolen for the purpose. Since the early Christians were forced to conceal their gatherings, meeting in secret, the conviction that they were engaged in shameful acts could seem plausible. In AD 177 in Lyons, a number of Christians were publicly tortured and killed by the Roman authorities, and these allegations played a large part in their condemnation. Some of those who died cried out denials of the accusations as they did so, evidence of the role the allegations had had in these horrible deaths.

When Christianity became the dominant religion in Europe, the idea of secret groups practising ritual murder did not disappear; Christian authorities took over the myth that had been used earlier to justify their own persecution. Like their Roman predecessors they used the accusation of ritual murder to denigrate and persecute opponents. In this case it was those divergent religious communities such as the Waldensians and the Cathars who were designated heretics, and accused of it. Centuries later, in a more elaborate development of the story, ritual murder was believed to be carried out by covens of witches, gathering to worship the Devil and feast on the flesh of human sacrifice. They represented the opposite of all that was considered good, their pleasure was believed to lie in doing evil and their aim was, ultimately, to destroy society. The rituals they performed were the opposite of Christian services: they took place at night, not in the daytime and in secret locations, not in public buildings that were known and open to all; most sinister of all, the rites included practices that represented all that was believed to be against human nature: cannibalistic feasts, incest and other perversions. It was these ideas that triggered the infamous witch-hunts of early modern Europe.

The picture I have drawn was built up gradually during the centuries, according to Cohn (1975). The people who were accused of ritual murder, or suspected if they were not accused, were people seen as non-believers, outsiders, whose very existence threatened the social fabric. Traditional healers, the wise men and women of mediaeval society, were also often accused. As Chapter 2 has described, belief in hidden conspiracies, secret societies whose members aimed to rule the world, were rife from the eighteenth century onwards (Parkin 1985).[11] Subsequently Jews, Freemasons, and, in twentieth century America, conspiracies of communists, were seen in a similar light, as people of evil intent, whose aim was to destroy society as it then existed. It is important to recognise the historical depth of our beliefs in a secret and conspiratorial group, the epitome of evil characterised by the ritual killing they are believed to indulge in. The depraved actions of these hidden beings are very similar to those of witches the world over: they commit incest, kill and eat human beings and commit the most lurid crimes. This is part of a cultural definition of evil, just as beliefs in witchcraft as a manifestation of evil are part of the worldview of most Africans.

The colonisation of Africa may have suppressed human sacrifice, but it allowed for the development in Europe of the myth of ritual murder in another direction. The former existence of human sacrifice in West Africa encouraged the most sinister beliefs about African culture. Events in Africa seemed to confirm these as realistic portrayals. From the end of the nineteenth century onwards there were outcrops of serial killings in different parts of Africa that local people claimed were the work of human beings who had transformed themselves into animals, usually leopards or lions. Given the belief that occurs in many parts of Africa that witches can transform themselves into wild animals for the purpose of killing and 'eating' other human beings, an anthropologist would expect that both the killing and the eating were spiritual rather than actual. However the deaths were real and the death blows appeared to have been dealt by an animal, showing wounds apparently inflicted by teeth and claws, although sceptics claimed that these mutilations might have been inflicted by special weapons designed to conceal the fact that the killer was another human being (Pratten 2007). In Sierra Leone, where the first such cases emerged, there were beliefs in the existence of secret societies of witches associated with leopards. It was thought that these societies might be to blame and that the killings were offerings to their secret shrines. Some witnesses claimed to have seen leopards attacking the victims, others claimed that the murderers were human beings disguised as leopards. The European colonial servants who were responsible for the areas in which these murders occurred and who shared to a greater or lesser extent existing fantasies about Africa, were unable to decide whether the killings were ritual murder or not. But reports of the deaths contributed to a whole genre of literature that embedded the notion of ritual murder ever more deeply into the European imagination.

Ritual murder is still murder and hence a crime. If we treat it as such, we have to consider what the evidence for it is. Over the course of history, many people have been accused of ritual murder and many have been executed for it, but the evidence for their guilt has been unsatisfactory from a modern point of view. Two kinds of evidence have been accepted as 'proof' of participation in ritual murder: first, accusations by people who claimed to have suffered the evil attacks and/or to have seen the secret evil-doing; and secondly, confessions from the accused, in former times often extracted by torture. Checks as to whether personal malice or pre-existing quarrels were the cause of accusations seem not to have been made, although the accused have often claimed that the allegations were the result of malice. Independent or material evidence such as would be demanded in a prosecution today has never existed. Yet the idea persists because it represents in a dramatic form what is the ultimate in inhuman evil and by contrast emphasises what it is to be human.

At the end of the twentieth century, people across the world asserted their belief in rituals that included the sacrifice of children as offerings to the devil. In the United States, Britain, Europe, Australia and New Zealand, similar accusations were made. The rituals were said to include a modern sin, that of the sexual abuse of children, but in other respects they resembled the accusations that had been made across early modern Europe, and included allegations of human sacrifice and cannibalism. But when investigated, the evidence that ritual murder was being perpetrated was very like that in early modern Europe: allegations, often from children and the 'confessions' of adults who claimed to have been participants. There was no forensic or material evidence.

Yet seven years after the ritual abuse panic died down in September 2001when a little boy's mutilated body was found floating in the Thames; some of the same people who had publicised their belief in Satanism claimed it as justifying their beliefs. The *Catholic Herald* proclaimed: 'Boy's torso prompts new "Satanic abuse" fears' (March 2002). Was this the proof of ritual murder that had not been available before? It was presented as such in the media (see Sanders 2003). According to one BBC News report, on 9 July 2002, police were investigating whether Adam's death 'was a West African voodoo killing involving human sacrifice'.

When it was discovered that the child Adam had probably been brought to London from Africa, which has for centuries been subject to myths about 'The Dark Continent', certain people hastened to claim that it 'proved' that human sacrifice was continuing to occur among the 'uncivilised'. This general attitude has been described very well by David Pratten, who wrote: 'Africa represented a blank space in Europe's collective imagination and could therefore be populated by all manner of invented creatures, sometimes noble, sometimes monstrous, that were the visual and visceral products of European fears and desires' (Pratten 2007: 9). Over-simplistic ideas about 'leopard societies' and secret organisations that kill for pleasure have also influenced some Christian missionaries in Nigeria and kept the idea of ritual murder alive.[12]

While Sanders has pointed out how the continued emphasis on the African provenance of 'ritual murder' has deepened existing prejudices about Africa and Africans, he stuffs all the evidence of British cultural concepts into that vast portmanteau labelled 'The Other'. Unfortunately this neither illuminates nor analyses the ethnographic material that is thus bundled together. It is important to show how British concepts of evil – particularly the ideas of ritual murder and human sacrifice – emerge in the way they think about African killings. 'Ritual murder' is a European representation of great evil; its origins have been uncovered by historians who have demonstrated its role in generating the Christian pursuit of witches in early modern Europe. Witches are no longer pursued and killed in modern Europe, although the myth of their presence and practices remains, surprisingly unchanged by time, and is manifest in secular as well as religious forms. Similarly, while it seems clear that human sacrifice is no longer practised in modern Africa, the conceptualisation of evil as witchcraft has survived the spread of the Abrahamic religions there. Like the myth of human sacrifice, ideas of witchcraft have been affected by historical events. In modern Africa, the Pentecostal belief in Satan's demonic servants as the source of the power of witchcraft is a new belief that ties the two concepts of evil firmly together into a single contemporary image of the grossest evil.

Notes

1 For the influence of the Nigerian film industry, see Pype 2009 and 2012.
2 Evans-Pritchard recorded that Nuer might offer a wild cucumber if no animal were available, but made it clear that this was merely a stand-in and embodied a pledge to perform the usual sacrifice of killing an animal when possible, preferably an ox. See Smith and Doniger 1989.
3 Speke records seeing the King of Buganda shoot the head off a passing slave to demonstrate to his European visitor the effectiveness of the guns he had bought from Arab traders. This clearly was not a sacrifice, though it was a demonstration of the Kabaka's power.
4 Given the pressure of the expectation of the husband's kin, and of society in general, it is hard to say that widows who committed 'suttee', as it was called, always died absolutely voluntarily.
5 Historians have pointed out that the fact of human sacrifice was used by some apologists for the slave trade to justify selling slaves because otherwise they might be taken for sacrifice (Law 1985).
6 This practice was recorded as far back as the seventeenth century.
7 This belief underlay the use in Europe of corpse medicine in which powdered human remains were used in healing, in a similar manner to that found in Africa today (see Sugg 2011).
8 The term denotes a concoction, made by specialists for their clients, which is magically rather than materially effective. It is thus not medicine in the modern Western sense, which is why I use the word in inverted commas. Law (1985) associates this practice with the results attributed to the eating of enemies' bodies in Old Calabar.
9 Killing was not always necessary; in Kenya recently two men have been arrested for dealing in body parts obtained from a crematorium.

10 It is worth noting that some of the allegations of Satan worshipping made at the end of the twentieth century repeated this triple evil, listing sexual orgies (including child sexual abuse), human sacrifice and cannibalism as acts performed in the rituals.

11 See the chapters by D. Pocock, D. Parkin and A. Macfarlane in Parkin 1985.

12 I think it no coincidence that Lawrence Pazder, author with Michelle Smith (his patient and later his wife) of *Michelle Remembers*, had once been a missionary in Nigeria. This book had a considerable influence in generating belief about satanic abuse in the United States in the 1980s.

Bibliography

Baaren, Th.P. van. 1964. 'Theoretical Speculations on Sacrifice', *Numen* 11(1) (January): 1–12.

Bohannan, P.J. (ed.). 1960. *African Homicide and Suicide*. Princeton, NJ: Princeton University Press.

Caplan, P. 2010. '"Child Sacrifice" in Uganda: The BBC, "Witch-doctors" and Anthropologists', *Anthropology Today* 26(2): 4–7.

Cohn, N. 1975. *Europe's Inner Demons*. St Albans: Paladin.

Kahaner, L. 1994. *Cults That Kill*. New York: Warner Books.

La Fontaine, J.S. 1998. *Speak of the Devil*. Cambridge: Cambridge University Press.

———. 1999. 'Satanism and Satanic Mythology', in *Witchcraft and Magic in Europe, Vol. VI. The Twentieth Century*, eds. Bengt Ankarloo and Stuart Clark. London: Athlone Press, pp. 83–139.

Law, R. 1985. 'Human Sacrifice in Pre-Colonial West Africa', *African Affairs* 84(334) (January): 53–87.

Macfarlane, A. 1985 'The root of all evil' in D. Parkin (ed.), *The Anthropology of Evil*. Oxford: Basil Blackwell, pp. 57–76.

Muchembled, R. 1990. 'Satanic Myths and Cultural Reality', in B. Ankarloo and G. Henningsen (eds), *Early Modern European Witchcraft*. Oxford: Clarendon Press, pp. 139–160.

Parkin, D. 1985. Introduction to D. Parkin (ed.), *The Anthropology of Evil*. Oxford: Basil Blackwell, pp. 1–25.

Pazder, L., and M. Smith. 1980. *Michelle Remembers*. New York: Pocket Books.

Pocock, D. 1985. 'Unruly Evil', in D. Parkin (ed.), *The Anthropology of Evil*. Oxford: Basil Blackwell, pp. 42–56.

Pratten, D. 2007. *The Man-Leopard Murders: History and Society in Colonial Nigeria* (International African Library). Edinburgh University Press.

Pype, K. 2009. 'Nollywood and Beyond', in M. Krings and O. Okoome, *Transitional Dimensions of the African Video Film Industry*. Proceedings of a symposium at the University of Mainz.

———. 2012. *The Making of the Pentecostal Melodrama: Religion, Media and Gender in Kinshasa*. New York: Berghahn Books.

Rives, J. 1995. 'Human Sacrifice among Pagans and Christians', *The Journal of Roman Studies* 85: 65–85.

Sahlins, M. 2003. 'Artificially Maintained Controversies: Global Warming and Fijian Cannibalism', *Anthropology Today* 19: 3–5.

Sanders, T. 2003. 'Imagining the Dark Continent: The Met, the Media and the Thames Torso', *Cambridge Anthropology* 23(3): 53–66.

Schmidt, B. 2009. 'The Practice of Spirit Possession in Haitian Vodou', in J. La Fontaine (ed.), *The Devil's Children: From Spirit Possession to Witchcraft, New Allegations that Affect Children*. Farnham: Ashgate, pp. 91–100.

Smith, Brian K. 2000. 'Capital Punishment and Human Sacrifice', *Journal of the American Academy of Religion* 68(1): 3–26.

Smith, Brian K., and Wendy Doniger. 1989. 'Sacrifice and Substitution: Ritual Mystification and Mythical Demystification', *Numen* 36(2) (December): 189–224.

Sugg, R. 2011. *Mummies, Cannibals and Vampires: The History of Corpse Medicine from the Renaissance to the Victorians*. London and New York: Routledge.

Chapter 4

MAGIC AND MEDICINE

The Torso in the Thames

This chapter starts with a real, not a hypothesised, murder of a child. On 21 September 2001, the body of a small black child, probably about five or six years old, was found floating in the Thames by Tower Bridge. The body, clothed only in a child's orange shorts, lacked a head, arms and legs which had been removed, leaving just the torso. The case, sometimes referred to as 'The Torso in the Thames', has evoked an extraordinary amount of interest and continues to do so. In a most unusual gesture, the police gave the remains a name, Adam,[1] which I shall use, although later it was claimed that his real name was Ikpomwosa.[2] The Metropolitan Police spent a large amount of time and resources on attempting to discover the identity of the child, and then who murdered him. They succeeded in the first task but not in the second. The inspector in charge, Will O'Reilly, has continued to hunt for Adam's killer, even after his retirement.[3]

My aim in discussing this case in detail is to demonstrate how cultural bias skews judgement. This is particularly the case when what is at issue is shocking or is considered to entail great evil. Secondly I want to show the strengths of anthropology's comparative method, using evidence from across cultures instead of trying to explain the meaning of a belief or practice by relying heavily on the analyst's own culturally determined 'meanings'.

This case has been widely accepted as an instance of human sacrifice (Hoskins 2012). The label evokes the myth discussed earlier in Chapters 2 and 3. It evokes the witches, servants of supreme evil, and contrasts them with the image of slaughtered innocence. In early modern Europe this myth was used to justify the torture and killing of large numbers of people who were accused of being witches. In its present form the evil has been attributed first to a secret cult of Devil worship (see Chapter 2) and then to Africa, and shows a similar power to reflect hostility against a whole category of people. It is another example of ethnocentric distortion of perception; in this instance it may have hampered police endeavours and has probably fuelled racist publicity. The results of informed comparison give us more reliable interpretations than relying on the nature of evil as depicted in our own culture's myths.

The police had some remarkable results to begin with. Despite having little to go on, their forensic experts discovered that the child was Nigerian; investigation showed that he had been brought to England via Germany, where the shorts on the body had been bought. The police traced a woman who admitted bringing him from Germany to England.[4] She was arrested, but later released because there was evidence to show her to have been in Germany at the time of the murder. She stated that she had handed the child over to other people in London whom she did not know. Whatever else has been found out, there has been no conclusive evidence to prove why or by whom he was killed.

In the popular mind as reflected in the media generally, the Torso in the Thames case was associated with ideas of barbarism and ancient African savagery, as Sanders (2003) rightly pointed out. While I agree with much of what he wrote, it remains to be explained why the idea of 'darkest Africa' was so widely accepted. To start with, it seems likely that because the concept of human sacrifice is an intrinsic part of a Christian concept of supreme evil, this particular incident has been taken without question as an instance of this. The rise of Christian fundamentalism in recent decades has brought the issue of combating evil to the fore. Whether this influenced attitudes cannot be proved, but the killing was rapidly designated as a 'human sacrifice', and more killings were (wrongly) forecast. Journalists and police alike were convinced by the same idea that a generation before had activated the panic about the ritual abuse of children (La Fontaine 1998, and see Chapter 2). At that time, public concern was focused on the belief that Satanist cults practising human sacrifice were rife in Britain. Twenty-five years later, the cults and their human sacrifices were presented as African traditions that were being brought into Europe by African migrants. (The connection of this idea with antipathy to migration is obvious.) The killing of Adam became 'a sacrifice', and his killers 'worshippers of an alien god'.

The investigation took several wrong turns. Adam's death was first associated with another somewhat earlier killing of a girl in Holland, also said to be 'ritualistic'. But her murderer was identified and jailed, and the case proved not to have anything to do with ritual or sacrifice. A bit later, a sheet with an inscription and candles found on the banks of the Thames were associated in the press with Adam's death, but this 'ritual paraphernalia' turned out to be the remains of a wholly Christian thanksgiving celebration of a family member's escape from the disaster of the Twin

Towers in New York. The general view of the case remained unchanged. By the time another film was made about the case, ten years later, the main difference in its conclusions was the suggestion that Adam had been trafficked to London specifically to be the victim in a human sacrifice.

However, from a different, more comparative angle,[5] it is immediately clear that murders very like that of Adam's are not uncommon in Africa. This would appear to support the British view, except that it is equally clear that these murders are not sacrifices. They were first reported publicly in South Africa. A spate of killings in the Northern Province occasioned the setting up of a commission that reported in 1996,[6] five years before Adam's death. It consisted of eight original members, all but one of black African birth, and was chaired by the late Professor N.V. Ralushai, a South African anthropologist of wide experience in Africa who had been trained at Queen's University Belfast. The commission's remit was to cover all forms of killing that involved magic or witchcraft, so their report (Ralushai 1996)[7] also contains accounts of witches being publicly killed by mobs of young people, primarily young men. These lynchings are quite distinct from the other murders which were committed secretly by unknown killers, who mutilated the body. The commission's report, based on a very large number of interviews, contains a wealth of information and some photographs of corpses lacking various body parts. It was these latter murders that resembled the case of Adam. The killings are known widely in South Africa by the Zulu term *muti*. In the report it was stated that in the Northern Province the Zulu word was not used, but since it was so current in the media and courts (in later years they might have included the international media as well), it had been decided to use it. The Metropolitan Police concerned with the Adam case visited South Africa and consulted police there, but did not appear to have been influenced by this report. Perhaps they considered the fact that the child was shown to be Nigerian, not South African, as meaning that these practices did not occur[8] in Nigeria or to Nigerians. What they, and others, failed to take into account was the widely disseminated reports of similar killings in Tanzania (mainly of albinos) and Uganda, and the fact that radio, television and a lively press ensured that information about this type of killing was spread through most of Africa. There have been some similar killings in Nigeria, though less widely reported. Thus the African origin of the crime against Adam would seem to have been substantiated by this data, but with a completely different meaning.

One prominent interpretation of the British crime, which exemplifies how ethnocentrism determined understandings of what had happened, was that of Richard Hoskins,[9] who was consulted by the police among others. His view, repeated in interviews and in a subsequent book,[10] was that the killing was a human sacrifice. He announced this before adducing evidence, but claimed that the body was 'drained of blood' (as well as having been mutilated, the body had been in the Thames for several days). Later he listed other characteristics that he asserted were common to sacrifices in Nigeria and the killing of Adam: 'the meticulous nature of the crime; the clothing of a particular colour; and the disposal of the torso in a flowing river' (Hoskins 2012: 89). Descriptions by historians of the human sacrifices in Benin and other kingdoms of the West Coast of Africa in earlier times do not support these conclusions.[11] Nor do anthropologists specialising in that area. What was not remarked by Hoskins was that the bodies of human sacrifices in West Africa were left whole.

Traces of the Calabar bean had been found in Adam's stomach in forensic investigation. It seems to have been used in a substance concocted for trials by ordeal, in which the accused is forced to drink a poisonous liquid whose ingredients include this bean. If death occurs subsequently it is considered as proof of guilt; if the accused survives, he, or more usually she, is proved innocent, but this happens infrequently. In a weaker solution it might also be used as a sedative. It is not clear why it had been used in this case: whether the child was accused of witchcraft or merely sedated.[12] Hoskins remarked that it was used by witchdoctors.

The Metropolitan Police had long decided that Adam's killing was a human sacrifice,[13] so they then searched for cults that might be performing human sacrifice. A member of the police team asked the assistant director of the charity 'Inform'[14] for the names of leaders of Aladura,[15] which he was convinced might be the cult [sic] he was looking for. He had also, he said, consulted with Professor John Peel, who had been unable (not surprisingly) to help him. Other than that request for information, the Metropolitan Police seemed to have avoided advice from those who might have helped them most. Sanders, in the article already cited, asked why the anthropologists who offered their services were ignored. He wrote: 'Do we offer a message that they do not want to hear, while others will offer interpretations that are closer to what they want to think?' The answer, as in the case discussed in the previous chapter, must be an unequivocal 'Yes'.

Before proceeding to consider why certain answers may be preferred, let us consider the nature of what investigators rejected, but which seems the most likely explanation: that is the *muti* murders. The best source of information available is the report of the Ralushai Commission (1996), but there are a number of media reports, such as on the killing of albinos in Tanzania and children in Uganda, to which reference can be made. Ralushai points out that the word *muti* can be translated as either 'magic' or 'medicine'. This conjunction of meanings associates two ideas that are now distinct in English culture but, as was revealed later, this was not always the case. This double meaning is important to any understanding of the practice of *muti*. Some extreme forms of *muti* make use of human body parts as ingredients in concoctions that were believed to be particularly powerful charms, designed to endow their possessor with wealth and general prosperity; other, lesser, charms did not. The term itself covers all forms of *muti*, not merely its more murderous ones.

According to Professor Ralushai's commission, murder was the means whereby the important ingredients of the most powerful *muti* were provided. Its very thorough investigation provided a list of human parts that were commonly removed from a corpse for use in this powerful magic described as 'for financial gain and to bring luck' (Ralushai 1996: 24–25, 255) – these were: the fat, skull, hands, eyes, blood, genitals, breasts and bones. Their uses as described in the report clearly owe their power to what Sir James Frazer would have called 'sympathetic magic': eyes to give far-sightedness, the genitals to promote fertility, blood to increase vitality, and so on. What is notable, however, is that, as in the case of Adam, although the soft external parts of the body might be excised, no internal organs were used.[16] The disposal of the body subsequently had no ritual or magical significance.

According to the Ralushai commission, *muti* are used by 'business people, inyangas (healers or magicians) and traditional leaders', who are the most usual clients for this kind of medicine, though they also reported that some church members were said to use it (Ralushai 1996: 25). It is important to note that the report writes of *muti* as being 'used' – not the sort of term that is chosen to describe the performance of ritual, whether including a sacrifice or not. The people who make and sell this medicine are mostly traditional healers. Its purposes to increase wealth and power are clear, but the healers who deal in this kind of *muti* also prepare mixtures for curing illnesses and preventing misfortune. In this aspect of their activities they resemble the 'wise men' and 'wise women' who were common targets of allegations of witchcraft in early modern England as described by the historians Keith Thomas (1971) and Alan Macfarlane (1970, 1985). It was in part to counter them, and bring people to rely on the Church and its prayers instead, that the witch-hunt was unleashed on Europe.

We have reached the point at which an answer to the question of whether *muti* is sacrifice or magical medicine can be reached. The detailed evidence set out here supports the conclusion that *muti* is magic. Here it is worth remembering that one of the founders of anthropology, Sir Edward Tylor, labelled magic a primitive form of science, rather than seeing it as a precursor of religion, as other early anthropologists did.

Marcel Mauss, following later, distinguished magic clearly from religion by pointing out that magic usually benefited individuals, was not the subject of communal acts and depended not on the existence of spirits, gods or ancestors but on the inherent power of the ingredients of the magic. While the field research of later anthropologists has documented cases of communal rituals that seem very magical in their construction, such as those for rain or bountiful harvests, the distinction between magic as private, practical and individual, and religion as public, addressed to spiritual beings and directed towards the common good, has largely survived in anthropology.

It was noted early in anthropology's history that herbal medicines, both in Europe and elsewhere, used what were believed to be the inherent powers of the plants, seeds and other ingredients of which they were made. These powers were not tested in ways that would satisfy modern chemists or physicists but were validated by belief, tradition and experience. Some ingredients of Western medicine, such as quinine, have since been derived from some of these herbal medicines. Other ingredients, however, were not validated by Western science and were thus labelled as magical in their effects. Such distinctions of course had no meaning to those who made and sold *muti*. The use of body parts that require murder to provide them is, of course, kept particularly secret, as it is both illegal and considered highly immoral by most Africans, although they might not deny that it does happen.

The Ralushai Commission noted that some people they interviewed stated that human fat and even body parts were obtainable from shops dealing in herbs in Johannesburg, but it is also true that no one who has said this has been able or willing to identify any of these shops. Hoskins implies that human body parts were being offered for sale in a Durban market he visited (2012: 11), but he did not actually see any. Most anthropologists would conclude that these stories are just that – stories or urban myths, which are common in many parts of the world. The Ralushai Report contains a photograph of the contents of a healer's pharmacopoeia that includes severed fingers (photo 11) but they were cut from the hand of a known victim, for whose murder the healer, who owned the contents of the basket, was identified and convicted. It does not seem that the fingers were for sale or that he usually sold body parts. It is much more likely, as was implied by much of the commission's information, that body parts were obtained when the magician had a customer who had paid for the costly *muti* that uses these ingredients. Investigations into the killings in Tanzania suggested that this is also what happened there.

South Africa is not the only place in Africa where such murders for medicine take place. Similar killings and mutilations have been reported further north in Tanzania, where albinos, particularly women and children, have been and still are targeted. The selection of albinos seems likely to have a similar explanation to the one that the Ralushai Commission was given for the (very rare)[17] use of white body parts: that the financial strength of whites and their [political and financial] power made their body parts a particularly strong ingredient in *muti*.

Some years later than the reporting of the murder of albinos, reports in Uganda focused on the murder and mutilation of children and a public panic ensued, as noted in the previous chapter. The BBC Newsnight 'documentary' on the issue filmed in Uganda presented the view that the killings were sacrifices offered to evil spirits.[18] In both places there were real killings and bodies were mutilated, but some victims were left alive, after limbs – and on one occasion, genitals – had been severed. The purpose of these acts was said by local people to be to obtain ingredients for powerful magic, as in South Africa.

The most recent discovery of the use of human flesh in medicine was made in 2012 in Korea, where capsules containing powdered human flesh have been discovered by Customs officials in travellers' baggage and in consignments of goods from China (BBC News, 7 May 2012). Pictures of the brightly coloured capsules accompanied the description of them as designed to improve the health, vitality and success of those who took them. As with contemporary Africa, probably only the rich can afford to use such capsules.

The use of human body parts in magic or medicine is reminiscent of a widespread medical practice that was actually found throughout Europe up until the mid to late nineteenth century, depending on location (Sugg 2011: 265–272) and as this recent information implies, elsewhere until the present day. The history of 'corpse medicine',[19] as it was called in English, goes back to classical antiquity. The use of human blood and organs, particularly the liver, was controversial to many at that time; some of the classical medical authorities found the procedures disgusting, although they might not dispute the efficacy of the treatment. By the Middle Ages though, the powdered flesh of ancient mummified corpses had been firmly established in Europe as a powerful, though costly, ingredient in medicine. The term for it was *mummia* or *mummy*, for these human substances include not only the flesh of embalmed bodies found in the tombs of the Egyptians, but also of the mummified bodies of unfortunate travellers who had died in the deserts and whose bodies had subsequently been desiccated by natural forces. Powdered bones and skulls were also considered effective in treating a number of ailments and in healing wounds. In 1618 the English College of Physicians listed mummy and blood in its official pharmacopoeia (Gordon-Grube 1993: 405).

At the other end of the seventeenth century, William Salmon, in his book published in 1763[20] and entitled *The Compleat English Physician or the Druggist's Shop*, lists several varieties of mummy from desiccated to 'modern', by which he means recently killed (see also Gordon-Grube 1993). Interestingly Salmon, described on the frontispiece as a 'Professor of Physick', prefers 'modern' mummy, which he claims not only has the advantage of being more easily obtained, but contains more of the Salt and Mummial Balsam than can be found in 'long-buried mummial carcases' (Salmon 1693: 713, section V).

In parallel to the use of corpse medicine there was a firm belief in the inherent power of blood, particularly if taken from a live or newly dead person, or from someone brave and strong. This is certainly a survival of the Roman remedy for epilepsy which entailed drinking the blood and/or consuming the liver of gladiators killed in public contests. Blood was recommended as a remedy for epilepsy as late as 1747 (Gordon-Grube 1993: 406). In early modern Europe, drinking blood was also widely considered to be an effective means of rejuvenating the old. Sugg (2011: 17) records a story that in 1492 Pope Innocent VII paid three youths to supply him with blood in an attempt to stave off his death. The young men were bled to death but the treatment failed. Blood (though given in transfusions and not drunk) is still a reputable treatment for some conditions. In October 2012, *The Guardian* newspaper reported an experiment on mice at the Stanford Medical School that concluded that transfusions of the blood of a young mouse into an old one had significantly retarded the ageing process, and had enhanced both memory and learning in the older one.[21]

The use of blood in love potions goes back to the Romans too (Sugg 2011: 278) and its use in pacts of friendship is also a long-standing tradition in Europe. Blood might be taken fresh or distilled in various ways, and mummy, skulls and other bones were powdered to use in medicine, which might either be in the form of an ointment or taken internally (see Salmon 1693: 713–15, Sections VI, VII and X). It was the rise of Paracelsian medicine, as well as the increasing scarcity of mummified corpses, that encouraged the use of fresh corpses, which might be supplied by executioners or gathered from the battlefields. In addition, skulls and the moss that grew on them were important sources of medical ingredients. A portrait of John Tradescant the Younger in the National Portrait Gallery[22] shows him with a mossy skull on the table before him. Corpse medicine seemed to have stopped short of murder, which was largely unnecessary as the corpses of criminals were available and plentiful. Presumably blood, as recorded in classical times, in Christian Europe and continuing to the present day, has always been available from donors at a price. Graves might also be robbed for their contents and all the ingredients needed by the healers were on sale.

Unlike the situation in contemporary Africa, where we do not know what the makers of *muti* think about the rationale underlying their use of human body parts, the theories behind the use of corpse medicine in Europe are freely available in the writings and disputations of the learned physicians and surgeons who wrote about their treatments. It was they whose work formed the basis of the newly emerging sciences of human physiology and anatomy. Their discussions revealed much about how corpse medicine was regarded, although great care must be exercised when using them to interpret behaviour outside Europe.

Sugg argues that corpse medicine was encouraged in early modern Europe by developments in Christian theology. It was generally believed that all reality was spiritual and came from God. This applied particularly to the human ingredients of medicine since humanity was the finest of His creations and human bodies were particularly potent (Sugg 2011: 173). He notes a distinction that developed between the south, in what would eventually be Catholic Europe, and the future Protestant populations of more northern countries.[23] This difference turns on the nature of the soul's connection with the body and what happens to both at death. In the south it was believed that at death the soul left the body instantly, leaving human remains deprived of life. In the north, however, the soul was believed to be linked to the body through spirits that infused every part of it, but were located particularly in certain organs and in the blood. The body's spirits were thought to be responsible for the body's functioning, and represented life itself. At death, while the soul left the body, the spirits remained in it for a period, the length of which differed according to the different experts. Death was a process rather than an event and the spirits of the body might be captured and used to heal a variety of conditions if the body parts used were taken from a recently dead person.

This historical evidence has also made apparent that observation and experience did lie behind much of the work of physicians who made use of corpse medicine. For example it was accurately observed that death by violence has an effect on the blood of the corpse. Modern science has shown that in such situations the extreme stress suffered by the victim triggers the secretion of anti-coagulants into the blood so that it remains liquid for much longer than usual after the person's death (Thorne 1997: 228, cited in Sugg 2011: 187). Thus the specification that blood be taken from a man who has died by violence,[24] either executed or in mortal combat, was based on experience of the extra liquidity of the blood, facilitating its drinking by the patient. However, the earlier explanation was the idea that the spirits were still present in it. In addition it must be remembered that dissection, which was already being practised by anatomists in medieval times, provided them with a wealth of information about the organs of the body. Perhaps the use of internal organs, such as the liver, heart and brain, in corpse medicine was related to these developments in the science of anatomy.[25]

Side by side with the physical observations that underpinned corpse medicine was a conviction in its effects that can now only be called magical. For example, the treatment of age by the infusion of the blood of youths could manifestly only retard the natural process of ageing by magical means, since the blood that was drunk would be digested by the body like any other food. Interestingly, as one effect of the revolution in thinking brought about by the emphasis on rationality, corpse medicine started to be denigrated as superstition – the folk medicine of the uneducated. Belief in it was projected into the past and envisaged as having been superseded by a medicine that was based on rational thought and the information supplied by science rather than magic, which directly parallels the dismissal of witchcraft by later scholars.

It may be significant that at a very early period international trade in 'mummy' had developed. Networks of traders were set up and in Britain taxes on the import of mummy were levied. Trade extended to the Far East,[26] with mummy being traded in the ships of the Dutch East India Company round the Cape of Good Hope to Japan. There is no evidence that Africa was or was not linked into this trade, but since they were involved in the trade of commodities both across the Sahara and by sea it does seem unlikely that the trade passed them by completely. As of now though, that is speculation.

The decline of corpse medicine is attributed by Sugg to several causes, including the rise of Enlightenment attitudes and the development of a scientifically based medicine used by the educated elite. He points out that the use of elements of 'corpse medicine' lingered on in popular medicine long after most physicians had abandoned it. Isolated instances of the use of blood, particularly in love magic and of human fat in candles, can be found until the twenty-first century. Bizarrely, one use for human fat was as fuel; until 2008 a Californian lipo-suction expert ran two cars, his own and his girlfriend's, on human fat drawn from his patients.[27] One colleague from a European country, with whom I was discussing this, immediately reminded me that the human placenta had been incorporated in various cosmetic creams. She added that in her country the umbilical cord was used in some manner to try to increase fertility, though she did not know exactly how.

While much popular medicine was increasingly dismissed by the educated as magic, and even denigrated as witchcraft or sorcery, what is clear is that, although the sceptics and opponents of its use expressed disgust as well as a lack of belief in its efficacy, it was not suggested that the use of the human body in this way was evil in itself. Of course the magic of 'wise' men and women was often what got them pursued as witches during the early modern witch-hunts, but by the eighteenth and nineteenth centuries that hysteria had mostly died down. The later association of some forms of corpse medicine with black magic and witchcraft manifestly classed corpse medicine as wicked, but its use never became a symbol of evil in the way that human sacrifice did. Sugg sees in the recurring idea (he calls it a fantasy) that 'the powerful will kill you to use your body for medical ends' (2011: 265) one form of the survival of corpse medicine. In *muti* we find one apparent realisation of a similar myth.

The use of human body parts in medicine in Africa resembles corpse medicine. But the term *muti* and its cognates in other languages encompass more than the English term 'medicine', for they cover not only forms of popular medicine used in combating illness but also the magic designed to make users of it more successful and more powerful. By contrast, drinking the blood of the young and courageous to rejuvenate the old was seen as purely physical in its effects; there seem to have been no claims in Europe that corpse medicine could enable an ordinary man to become rich or endow him with power. Unlike *muti* or the Chinese capsules, corpse medicine did not promise success or power.

Two other differences stand out. To start with, the purveyors of corpse medicine used the bodies of those who were already dead – in the case of the mummified bodies of Egyptians or desert travellers they were long dead. Even where fresh corpses were said to be necessary, as Paracelsus and his followers believed, there were plentiful supplies of the bodies of soldiers who died in the frequent and bloody battles of the time or of felons who had been hanged or executed for their crimes. There were, across the centuries, the occasional murders – mostly so that the victim would provide the murderer with human fat, but they were rare; the last of these was recorded in the United States in 1957. Most corpse medicine in earlier years was provided by the already dead. The African healers by contrast deliberately kill, or pay to have killed, those who supply them with body parts; the only exceptions known to me are represented by two Kenyans who developed a trade in parts removed from corpses sent to the crematorium.

A final difference is that corpse medicine used the hearts, livers and brains of the dead as well as their limbs, skulls and blood. *Muti* seems commonly to restrict its use to the external parts of the body, with the exception of human fat. Some healers may shave off body hair, even eyebrows, to use. Body hair is also used in sorcery. We may interpret that to mean that since hair grows after death it may be considered to contain particularly strong bodily powers. Children are frequent victims; this may be because they are easier to overpower or it may be because their youth implies a potential for growth which can be harnessed in the medicine made from their remains. It has been recorded that circumcised children have escaped being murdered for *muti*, which implies that bodily integrity is significant – 'Adam', however, was circumcised. Rationales probably vary from place to place and from one healer to another. But by the time Europeans brought their understanding of medicine to Africa it no longer included corpse medicine, and African usages were not widely recorded.

The murders for *muti* clearly resemble, if not exactly, the use of the human body for medicine for several centuries in Europe. But the police[28] and the media quite quickly assimilated the murder of Adam to the Western moral notion of extreme evil, labelling it human sacrifice. The labels ritual killing, voodoo and human sacrifice were bandied about between journalists with what often seemed like ghoulish glee when they wrote about the death of Adam. Ronke Phillips, the half-Nigerian journalist for ITV's *London Tonight*, who made a film about the case, published an accompanying article that drew every last drop of horror out of imagining the child's death. Her article was illustrated by the face of an angelic child that has subsequently (and wrongly) been taken to be Adam[29] – the image of innocence showing in stark relief the evil of his killers.

In Europe the preferred interpretation of these practices is as human sacrifice; they are interpreted as religious rites and may be attributed to a 'cult' assembling its members to perform the ritual. The practical purposes are not completely ignored but, on the pattern of Christianity, they are seen as being achieved through the mediation of a divine or spiritual power, in such cases an alien and evil one. 'Human sacrifice' is a phrase that incorporates all that is forbidden,[30] but also all that does not pertain to present-day society, only to alien and distant peoples. Clearly, the 'interpretations that are closer to what they want to think' centre on the worship of strange gods by this murderous evil act.

Of course, in some contexts, the law for example, it does not matter why Adam was killed. Murder is murder, no matter what the motive, though perhaps murder of a child by a rich man to increase his power is more distasteful than most killings. However for anthropologists the way in which the event was regarded in Britain is of interest, as it demonstrates how British culture has been shaped by Christian thought, despite the documented decline in Christian worship. The rise of fundamentalist Christianity, in which a preoccupation with evil and its eradication is characteristic, has given new life to the forms in which that evil is seen (see Gold 2009). Its influence can be seen in the fact that exorcism is now widely practised, which was not so fifty years ago. We should take the ideas accepted by the Metropolitan Police, and publicised by Hoskins, as ethnographic evidence rather than valid conclusions about the nature of the case.

There is a further question raised by the case of Adam's murder for anthropologists, who must consider how ethnocentric they still are. Are they influenced by concepts and ideas of which they are not fully aware, and their thinking limited by assumptions that are culturally specific? One of them, the belief that Western society is different in kind from others, is extraordinarily misleading, as my brief description of corpse medicine has tried to show. Sugg's book was a shock to me, as it was to many others, including some professional historians, his colleagues. However it supports the argument that comparison with other societies before conclusions are drawn is vital, and makes clear that this must be a comparison of acts, of behaviour as well as symbols, rather than solely motives and meanings that are inferred rather than documented. When we have established authentic ethnographic parallels in other societies we can use them to understand events nearer at hand. Adam's case has exemplified how untrained judgements are affected by cultural bias. It would be of benefit to the communities we live in if they could accept that our training is a qualification that makes anthropologists' views more useful than 'the ones they want to hear'.

Notes

This chapter is based on a paper given to the Anthropology Department of Unversity College London. I am grateful for the invitation and the useful discussion that followed.

1   Todd Sanders first remarked on this unusual gesture in his article 'Imagining the Dark Continent: The Met, the Media and the Thames Torso' (2003).

2   This was announced in a programme on the subject made by ITV for London Tonight (9 April 2011). More recently, the BBC reinterviewed the person who had supplied this name and she gave him a different name: Patrick Erhabor (BBC Two, 7 February 2013). However I shall continue to use the name Adam since it was under this name that the murder victim became a creature of myth.

3   A lecture on the case was given at the Child Exploitation and Online Protection (CEOP) Intelligence and Training Unit of the Metropolitan Police on 6 September 2012. One of the presenters was Will O'Reilly.

4   The reliability of this witness has been increasingly called into question.

5   It has been put to me that the amputations might simply have been the killer's device to avoid detection, but the fact that neither the head nor any of the severed limbs were recovered is unusual. I think it unlikely that this was an 'ordinary' murder.

6   It was submitted to the Hon. members of the Executive Council for Safety and Security in the Province.

7   My thanks to Professor Ralushai, who kindly sent me a copy of his report.

8   They cannot have visited Prof. Ralushai or seen his report, or the similarities must surely have struck them.

9   A former lecturer at Bath Spa University who had served in a Baptist mission in the Congo, and has both a BA and a Ph.D. in theology.

10 This book has subsequently been publicly repudiated by the police as inaccurate and lacking in integrity, at a conference in Nottingham in 2013. Also D.I. (ret'd) W. O'Reilly personal communication, 6 September 2012.

11 Nor, as far as I can find out, from colleagues who have worked in Nigeria, do those of modern Nigerian sacrifices of animals. One of them dismissed the 'evidence' as 'pure invention'.

12 The work of charities such as AFRUCA has established the fact that children accused of witchcraft may be rejected by their kin, who then become street children who are vulnerable to traffickers who may 'sell' them for various purposes.

13 In his book, Hoskins records that he persuaded Commander Andy Baker of this. This was denied by the Met. The book was publicly denied to be an account of the case by Baker and O'Reilly.

14 A charity associated with the London School of Economics that collects reliable information on new religions. I was present at the discussion.

15 Aladura is the name given to a group of African-initiated Christian churches. They are distinguished by wearing white clothes to their services, signifying the purity and equality of all members, and for emphasising prayer as the only means to make use of divine power. The term is not the name of a single organisation, nor is it a 'cult'. This information did not seem to be welcome.

16 This is contrary to what Richard Hoskins states in discussing this case (2012: 14, 25). In some areas the heart might be removed but there are few reports of that. It must also be remembered that the practice of *muti* might involve different ideas about the body and its powers in different parts of Africa.

17 Only two cases in the whole of South Africa of the killing and mutilation of whites for *muti* were given by the commission (Ralushai 1996: 25)

18 This is not a practice that has been recorded as occurring anywhere else in Africa.

19 I take this account largely from *Mummies, Cannibals and Vampires* by the historian Richard Sugg (2011). It gives a comprehensive account of this type of medicine from its inception, its use in medieval Europe and its rise to popularity in the Renaissance until its demise among the poor in Victoria's reign. Sugg also makes interesting connections between the use of corpse medicine, magic and witchcraft that I have found very stimulating. He is not responsible for the use I have made of his work.

20 The Compleat English Physician has three pages on the different forms and uses of mummy, both desiccated and fresh by William Salmon, the author. I am most grateful to Professor Paul Cullinan of Imperial College London who owns a copy of this interesting work, for allowing me to make use of it.

21 Similarly the blood of an old mouse accelerated the ageing process in a young one (*The Guardian*, 17 October 2012).

22 The portrait appears on the cover of Sugg's book, and I have seen it in the National Portrait Gallery where it is hung with portraits of other savants of the age.

23 However, Gordon-Grube (1993: 405) states that corpse medicine was not officially countenanced in the American Colonies, which seems an odd contradiction since the

colonies were nothing if not reformist in their religion, and the Rev. Taylor who prepared a pharmacopoeia, including mummy, in the mid seventeenth century was emi-
nently respectable.

24   As Salmon states in his pharmacopoeia, p. 713, section V.

25   This is my speculation and should not be held against Dr Sugg.

26   Dr R. Sugg, personal communication.

27   Reported by Sugg (2011: 284). In 2008, the Californian was found to be guilty of infring-
ing the laws regarding human tissues, and went into hiding.

28   Of course Dr Sugg's book was not published until 2011, although he cites a much earlier
article on the subject by Karen Gordon-Grube.

29   In fact the picture of him appearing briefly in the film was not, to my mind like this photograph, which shows a younger, better dressed, better fed and happier child. I wrote
this last sentence before reading that in the recent (2013) BBC account of the case, this
child was identified as Danny, who is alive and living in Germany. He was interviewed
for the BBC programme and recognised his photograph.

30   See article 5 in this volume.

Bibliography

Gold, M. 2009. 'Possession and Deliverance in a British Pentecostal Church', in J. La Fontaine
(ed.), *The Devil's Children: From Spirit Possession to Witchcraft, New Allegations that Affect
Children*. Farnham: Ashgate, pp. 61–76.

Gordon-Grube, K. 1988. 'Anthropophagy in Post-Renaissance Europe: The Tradition of
Medicinal Cannibalism', American Anthropologist 90: 405–9.

———. 1993. 'Evidence of Medicinal Cannibalism in Puritan New England: "Mummy" and
Related Remedies in Edward Taylor's "Dispensatory"', Early American Literature 28(3):
195.

Hoskins, R. 2012. *The Boy in the River*. Basingstoke and Oxford: Pan Macmillan.

La Fontaine, J.S. 1998. *Speak of the Devil*. Cambridge: Cambridge University Press.

Macfarlane, A. 1970. *Witchcraft in Tudor and Stuart England: A Regional and Comparative Study*.
London: Routledge & Kegan Paul.

———. 1985. 'The Root of All Evil', in D. Parkin (ed.), *The Anthropology of Evil*. Oxford:
Blackwell, pp. 57–76.

Ralushai, N.V. 1996. 'Report of the Commission of Enquiry into Witchcraft, Violence and
Ritual Murders in the Northern Province of the Republic of South Africa'. Unpublished
manuscript.

Salmon, W. 1693. *The Compleat English Physician or the Druggist's Shop Opened*. London:
Gillyflower and Sawbridge.

Sanders, T. 2003. 'Imagining the Dark Continent: The Met, the Media and the Thames Torso',
Cambridge Anthropology 23(3): 53–64.

Sugg, R. 2011. *Mummies, Cannibals and Vampires: The History of Corpse Medicine from the
Renaissance to the Victorians*. London and New York: Routledge.

Thomas, K. 1971. *Religion and the Decline of Magic*. London: Weidenfeld & Nicholson.

Thorne, A. 1997. *Countess Dracula: The Life and Times of the Blood Countess, Elisabeth Bathory*.
London: Bloomsbury.

Chapter 5

CHILD WITCHES IN LONDON
Tradition and Change in Religious Belief

On 3 June 2005 at the Old Bailey, two women and a man, all from Angola, were convicted of cruelty to an eight-year-old girl.[1] The child was in the care of one of them, a woman who claimed to be her mother, although DNA tests subsequently revealed her to be a more distant relative. The household contained another woman, not apparently related, and her son. The victim (referred to throughout as 'Child B' to maintain her anonymity) had been accused of being a witch, initially by the child of the other woman. She was grossly abused by the adults and only saved from death by drowning by the boyfriend of one of the women, who had argued that the British police would doubtless find out who had killed her. The maltreatment – starvation, beatings, cuts made on her chest, and chilli pepper[2] rubbed in her eyes – were attempts, it was alleged, to force the devil responsible for her witchcraft to leave her body. This was the first time such beliefs and practices had been made public in the British press, although some five years earlier a girl of similar age, Victoria Climbié, had had deliverance ritual[3] performed for her by the pastor of the church she had attended, and had subsequently died at the hands of the woman she lived with, also a distant relative. In the case of Victoria Climbié the allegations of witchcraft or possession by demons were downplayed in the press accounts; in 2005 they were the central focus. By 2006, when Eleanor Stobart's report for the then Department of Education and Skills was published,[4] the existence of many more similar cases was revealed. In 2005 there had been some 18 cases in which children had been abused as a result of their having been considered to be possessed by an evil spirit or to be engaging in witchcraft against their accusers. This was nearly half the total number of cases studied by Stobart, who wrote that: 'even at the time of writing other cases are coming to light'.

A more recent and dramatic case kept the problem before the public eye. In 2012 during a trial that filled the British press, the tragic and distressing accounts of the suffering of a Congolese teenager, were published. Kristy Bamu was beaten and tortured by his sister's boyfriend following accusations of witchcraft and finally drowned in the bath of water he was dumped in, too injured to save himself by keeping his head above the water. Kristy and his siblings had come from Paris, where they normally lived with their parents, to spend the Christmas holiday in 2010 with their eldest sister, Magalie Bamu. She lived in London with her boyfriend, Eric Bikebi, also Congolese by origin, but who had grown up, largely in care, in London. On conviction, both of them were sentenced to long terms of imprisonment, leaving their two year old son to be taken into care, despite the wishes of his grandparents in Paris to give him a home with them.[5]

It seemed to be the general opinion that what was happening was that migrants from other countries had brought their traditional beliefs with them. There is, however, one major objection to this view. Traditional African beliefs in witchcraft did not usually associate children with the practice of witchcraft. Traditionally, they were victims, the vulnerable possessions of adults who might be attacked through them. In Uganda, where I worked in the 1950s, adults would have dismissed the idea of witchcraft by children, for they were not considered strong or knowledgeable enough to exercise such powers. This approach resembled that of the Azanda recorded by Evans-Pritchard in the 1930s, when he wrote that 'The witchcraft-substance of a child is so small that it can cause little injury to others. Therefore a child is never accused of murder and even grown boys and girls are not suspected of serious witchcraft' (Evans-Pritchard 1937: 31). This, as far as I know,[6] was the traditional pattern almost everywhere in Africa.

In 1970 Robert Brain, the first anthropologist to describe child witches, wrote of the Bangwa of Cameroon that children were accused of witchcraft and might confess to using it, giving the names of their victims. However, he also pointed out that 'most misfortunes are explained through the maleficence of *adult* witchcraft' (1970: 162, my emphasis) and he cites some evidence that the beliefs in child witches (ibid.: 178) were new. Accusations against children were linked, by his informants as well as by Brain, with the changes following colonialism, and with the gradual disappearance of beliefs in children being set apart as 'children of the gods'. 'Children of the gods' were affected by the gods of the earth to which they yearned to return in death.[7] They had the power to return to the world of unborn children if they wished it strongly enough, and their attachment to the earth was seen as fragile, so ritual treatment was required to keep them in the land of the living.

By contrast, 'children of the sky' were children supernaturally punished for the crime of witchcraft. Both were set apart from other children and were 'subject to mystical dangers that could only be removed through ritual' (Brain 1970: 162). The witchcraft of the 'children of the sky' was only a part of traditional Bangwa witchcraft. It might be displayed in a child's illness or shown by autopsy after a child's death. Children might also be implicated in the confessions of other witches, or their witchcraft might be detected by diviners. Their victims were usually close kin, but confession and the appropriate ritual were believed to cure both the sinner and the afflicted.

Child witches might have been a new phenomenon in Bangwa, but they were 'everywhere', wrote Brain. 'Witchcraft accusations and exorcisms were ten a penny' (1970: 178). One paramount chief called a meeting of experts to advise him on why this was so. Brain was also concerned to explain the increase, and particularly the increase in accusations against children, by association with rapid social change (ibid.: 177). He pointed out that although there had been a great deal of social and political change, there was no Christian mission in the area until the late 1960s. But, he remarked, missionaries appeared not to discourage the ideas of witch children as much as they did beliefs in 'children of the gods', which they classed as superstitions. On the other hand, wrote Brain, 'they are fascinated by witchcraft'. One priest gave people holy water to protect them against witchcraft, and another told of his having killed a witch that he found lurking round his house at night. Christianity might be presented as a weapon against evil, that was conceptualised by priests as a possessing demon, but in popular thought personified as a witch. Thus the earliest mention of child witches in the anthropological literature is accompanied by the implication that they owe their perpetuation, if not their origin, to a syncretism of Christian and African belief.

Little further was published until 1980 when Geschiere recorded a 'new type of child-witchcraft', mbati, which appeared among the Maka of south-eastern Cameroon in the 1970s but lasted only two or three years. It was said to have been adopted from the North; according to Geschiere, the Maka adopted ideas and beliefs from their neighbours and from Europeans with ease (Geschiere 1980: 270). Mbati attacked only virgin boys; those in the cases described by Geschiere were probably in their early teens. As his title 'Child Witches against the Authority of their Elders' indicated, Geschiere saw this as a symbolic rebellion against the authority of the traditional elders. He argued that the incidents concerning mbati should be compared to the witch-cleansing movements of Central Africa, whose members were also young. (The latter were, however, old enough to be characterised as men, and were identifying, rather than claiming to be, witches.)

The Maka boys had been 'given' their witchcraft by an unnamed other and no mention was made of possessing demons. Like the Bangwa children, they confessed to and elaborated on their wicked plans, claiming to be taking revenge on their parents for failure to feed them enough meat.[8] There was some competitiveness in the confessions of the boys who were the main actors in the case (Geschiere 1980: 281). Although the boys were not accused of causing the specific harm that had led to their detection, and did not confess to having harmed anyone in particular, the subsequent illness of the father of one boy led to the adults taking the matter seriously. Like the witchcraft that would later be linked to possession by the Devil or evil spirits, *mbati* required exorcism carried out by a specialist. This appears to have cured it. Geschiere concluded that this was a symbolic rebellion made possible by the fact that the elders' authority had already been seriously undermined by the colonial regime and by the introduction of a money economy (ibid.: 283). Thus he did not consider it to be the effect of Christian missionary activity, but explained it as an epiphenomenon of colonialism. A problem he leaves his readers with is that his analysis did not take into account the fact that the main challenge to the authority of the elders during the reported incident came from employees of the state who punished the boys by beating them, thus taking action out of the hands of the elders.[9]

Subsequent writing on the impact of Christianity on African religions (often referred to, inaccurately, in the singular) is largely agreed on its effects. To begin with, many missionaries, unlike those in Bangwa during Brain's field-work, denounced belief in witchcraft as pagan and as manifesting a lack of faith in the power of God. The majority of Africans found this hard to accept. Later, as is amply demonstrated by a whole plethora of writers, African and non-African, witchcraft was assimilated into ideas of the devil's work and, as Christianity offered no competing explanation of misfortune, beliefs in witchcraft survived. Among African Christians, witchcraft was established as the work of the devil, although Western missionaries might try to eradicate the belief altogether.

The rise of fundamentalist Christianity in the West at the end of the twentieth century, provide a solution to the African difficulties with Christianity by providing a bridge to the old ideas. The new Pentecostal and charismatic Christians who began proselytising in Africa at the end of the twentieth century[10] were preoccupied with fighting evil. Both the missionaries and their converts believed in the existence of Satan, the prevalence of devils, his servants in promoting evil, and in the use of demonic powers to practise witchcraft.

The African churches that sprang up under the influence of this fundamentalist Christianity, particularly the Pentecostal variety, naturally resembled Pentecostal churches in Britain and the US whose missions had inspired them. Many of these independent African churches now have congregations throughout the African diaspora, including London. Speaking in tongues, exorcism for possession by devils and belief in the power of witchcraft are characteristic of these African Independent churches. Moreover their focus on success, measured in wealth and possessions as the mark of God's favour, included the belief that those who did not succeed were prevented from doing so by witchcraft. De Boeck is definite: 'Beyond any doubt' the Pentecostal churches play a 'crucial' role in the production of the modern figure of the witch (2004: 173).

There seems to be no obvious doctrinal origin in any of these forms of Christianity for the belief that *children* are particularly vulnerable to possession by the devil and thereby gaining witchcraft powers. There is no discussion of original sin in the large literature about the new African churches, nor mention of the frailties of children making them more likely to be possessed of demons or to exercise the powers of witches, unlike Bangladeshis who, as Dein notes (2009: 81),[11] do think children are more vulnerable to possession by demons because of their weakness. Thus, while the surge of accusations of witchcraft in Kinshasa and even in London can be explained by the rise of the new African Christianity and its preoccupation with the Devil, the problem remains: why children? Why was there this major change of target for witchcraft accusations?

The explanations I have cited imply that the accusations follow after a change in 'religious belief'. Two of them, Brain and de Boeck, refer to the syncretism that followed the introduction of Christianity into Africa, but interestingly there was no immediate increase in witchcraft accusations. The (unintended) preservation of beliefs in witchcraft by the initial missionary endeavour did not provoke a rash of new accusations, nor were children accused. Other factors were clearly needed before children would be accused, and in very large numbers.

In Geschiere's account it was the allegation of a child who claimed to have been frightened by his peers to make him join them that brought their witchcraft to light. The accused children confessed to having accepted the offer to teach them *mbati*, a form of magical knowledge. The allegation was not taken seriously at first by the adults and none of the children were said to have been possessed by evil spirits or demons. By contrast in Kinshasa, and in the two cases in London with which this account started, it was adults seeking the cause of misfortune in their own households who identified children as harbouring the demons which had enabled them to inflict suffering upon their parents out of malice. This is the link between possession by demons and the power to harm others that is characteristic of the new evil-doing. It must be distinguished from the other phenomenon that has appeared in multi-ethnic London such as: children's possession by evil spirits without such concomitant powers.

Filip de Boeck, writing a generation after the first descriptions of child witches in Africa (de Boeck 2002, 2003, n.d. but introduction 2004; and see de Boeck 2009), has discussed the causes of the phenomenon in several publications. His view is that in central Africa there was a change in the whole concept of childhood. He attributed this to the results of violent upheavals in the area causing large numbers of deaths and displacement. In particular he emphasises the part played in this changed view by child soldiers, children who became diamond hunters, child prostitutes and children who survived in the streets without adult care. A report by Javier Aguilar Molina (n.d.) for the Save the Children Fund's office in Kinshasa supports this analysis, and both authors refer to thousands of children living on the street after having been rejected for being witches.

While similar cases of rejected children are now reported elsewhere in Africa,[12] the Democratic Republic of the Congo (DRC) was the earliest site of what might be called an epidemic of such accusations that spread through the Congo basin. The exact numbers of such children is uncertain but all estimates seem to be in the thousands. It is unlikely to be coincidental that 'Child B' and the people she lived with came from the Cabinda enclave which lies in this area. However, Victoria Climbié came from Ivory Coast and the latest severe epidemic of accusations of witchcraft against children has been reported in the Delta region of Nigeria, in Akwa Ibom State. This area, like that of the Congo basin, is inhabited by the poor and uneducated and has been devastated by rebellions, kidnappings and the uncertainties of political strife. It is reported, however, that many of the accusations in Akwa Ibom stem from the influence of one particular pastor, the founder of a Pentecostal church, who also makes religious videos (Foxcroft 2007). One of them in particular accuses children of responsibility for the sufferings of people in the region through their witchcraft and has been widely sold. A local charity that is struggling to look after children thrown out of their homes by parents who accuse them of witchcraft, holds her activities responsible for the children's plight.[13]

As de Boeck points out, the Christian church's involvement in the 21st century phenomenon of child witches goes beyond the mere provision of ideas that have been incorporated into the belief system of churches of African origin. He and Aguilar Molina make this clear. The pastors of African churches in Kinshasa can be seen to encourage accusations. They may be asked to diagnose the cause of the child's condition, or to confirm parental or other suspicions of witchcraft; they also expel the evil spirit responsible for the witchcraft. There is a suggestion that these prophets, as they are also called, obtain not only considerable material rewards, but the prestige of increasingly large congregations by their successful exorcisms, so that it is clearly in their interest to identify children as witches. Splits in congregations have created breakaway churches, resulting in more leaders available for consultation. Haynes (2012) described this process in churches in Zambia where, she reported, pastors were known to be vigilant during services lest members of the congregation show manifestations of the Holy Spirit that indicate a special status and possibly competition for leadership. The rapid spread of accusations could thus be said to be driven by competition among the leaders of the new churches (compare Gold 2009). In sum, we have a background of changed concepts, both of evil and of children, activated by religious entrepreneurs who encourage the diagnosis of witchcraft in the households of those who are searching for an explanation of their misfortunes. Such a clustering of factors can be found elsewhere in Africa and throughout the African diaspora; so too are accusations against children.

Child Witches in the African Diaspora

The activities of African churches in diagnosing and treating child witches continue in the African diaspora. De Boeck recounts (2004: 163) how he first became interested in the phenomenon, not in the DRC, but in Belgium, where he came across a video of the cross-examination of three Congolese children, who were accused of being witches. Recent reports on the phenomenon in the U.K. (for the Department for Education and Skills [DfES] published in 2006 and for the Metropolitan Police)[14] make clear that there have been a number of cases over and above those that reach the newspapers. The author claimed more were being reported all the time (see the version of Stobart's report published in La Fontaine 2009).

The particular factors that seem to have been involved in the DRC in creating an evil image of children are conspicuously absent in London. Yet, while perhaps they may be free of the effects of war, of epidemics and of fleeing from genocidal armed forces,[15] migrants to London may still suffer anxiety, poverty and distress. The need to find causes for failing to succeed even after having reached the promised land of a Western city may sustain beliefs in child witches as a threat to the households in which they live. Once formulated, and accepted, the changed view of children was not so easily abandoned.

The main church associated with the detection and exorcism of child witches in Kinshasa, Combat Spirituelle, has branches in London and many adherents among the large Congolese community there. Eleanor Stobart's study, commissioned by the DfES, mentions a 'significant cluster' (2006: 12) of cases from the Democratic Republic of the Congo,[16] and the importance of the phenomenon in the community has been confirmed by other individuals I have talked to. However, the problem is not confined to recent migrants; a sizeable proportion of the children in the cases studied by Stobart were born in the U.K.

For reasons both geographical and social, it is not possible (yet) for young children to survive on the street in Britain as they do in Kinshasa, although a few teenagers may do so. Those concerned with the problem point out that the accused children form a very small proportion of all children who are abused in Britain (e.g. Stobart 2006: 28; R. Pull 2009). There is only anecdotal evidence of one case in which children were kept on church premises until they were exorcised, as they may be in Nigeria; nor are children forced onto the street, although in some cases the adults responsible for the child have been recorded as asking social services to take him or her into care. One charity formed to help neglected and deprived children admitted that some of them have been virtually driven from home as a consequence of being accused of witchcraft. Some children have been repatriated to be exorcised and some seem to have been abandoned there (see Stobart 2006). One pastor was said to have encouraged parents to send their child back to Kinshasa where he would be killed. Another child apparently abandoned in Kinshasa has appeared in a TV documentary made by Richard Hoskins (Witch Child, BBC2, 6 April 2006). In general, however, the British problem is both less visible and much smaller than that in Kinshasa.

Street children in Kinshasa survive outside any domestic organisation and are subject to no parental or other authority, apart from occasional attacks on them by the police and sometimes by members of the public. To a large extent they can be said to be out of control and outside normal social life. It could be said that a similar problem exists in London. In recent years much attention has been paid by the media to children who are beyond parental control and who take drugs, drink alcohol, truant from school, steal and vandalise their environment and indulge in shocking, often random, violence. Remarks about the breakdown of society are made while the debate about how to get rid of the problem continues. These highly visible anti-social children represent in exaggerated, but all too credible form, the fears of many immigrant parents about what will happen to their children in this country. They are said to be shocked at the extent of unbelief among British adults, and view the society into which they have come as immoral and as one in which children are ill-disciplined by their parents, who allow immoral behaviour in their children as well. The police seem unable to exercise any control. To these immigrants, parents are prevented from exercising the punishments they expect to use in order to control their children and bring them up 'properly'. The present NSPCC campaign to make smacking illegal is seen as depriving parents of their natural rights. If the children who are difficult to control are also not closely linked to the adults by ties of blood, their relationships with the adults are further jeopardized. They fear that their own children, who may go to schools with these evil children, will be contaminated and grow up like them. Even those who do not accuse their children of witchcraft may send them back to their country of origin, where they can be disciplined and avoid the influence of their British contemporaries. Others see their children growing up like their British age-mates and when there is conflict about their behaviour, parents are afraid that the children may even be possessed by demons.

Another finding in Kinshasa is mirrored in contemporary London and that is the existence in some African households (how many, no one knows) of children who do not belong to its core family. They may be distant relatives, but often they are unrelated children who have been trafficked into Britain to do housework or as baby-sitters, to attract child benefits or in some cases to be forced to work as prostitutes or in other illegal enterprises such as the growing of cannabis (ECPAT 2006). 'Child B', in the case with which this account started, was living with a distant female kinswoman who had brought her to Britain. Victoria Climbié was killed by a distant 'aunt' (some say great-aunt) who had brought her from Ivory Coast. Stobart (2006) comments: 'it has become apparent that children including unaccompanied minors can travel internationally and nationally with considerable ease in a way that is very difficult to monitor. This lack of monitoring can increase their vulnerability' (ibid.: 25). These children will be the marginal members of the households in which they find themselves and like other survivors of displacement may well show the behavioural effects of their distress.

Possession by demons is not solely a Christian idea. However the beliefs in different religious systems are not identical. Some Pentecostal churches may believe in possession by demons but believe it to be confined to adults (see Gold 2009), while other religions believe in possession as a means of communication with the divine and induce it in their religious ceremonies (see Harrington 2009; Schmidt 2009). Some religious groups who do hold the idea of children's being possessed by demons do not associate this with their becoming witches and harming others, but as the cause of sickness and failure to thrive. Dein (2009) makes clear that this is the case among Bangladeshis in East London. A social worker who has had some experience of such cases informed me that in Asian families generally children might be believed to be possessed by evil spirits, but they were not usually witches. Another case described to me as being a matter of child witches in fact concerned children said to be endangered by the witchcraft of their parents' enemies – an older African idea.

The idea of children's using witchcraft may be being promoted by religious leaders, but little is known. Moreover, fear of a pastor's powers may prevent members of his congregation from testifying against him or her. In 2007,[17] the Reverend Tukala was not taken to court and charged with causing cruelty to children through accusing them of witchcraft. Despite investigation by the BBC News team and a video shown on television that showed him identifying witchcraft in the case of a very small boy, legally there was said to be no case. The witnesses had refused to testify. However since then the role of pastors in identifying children as witches has become clearer (see Chapter 8).

There are said to be fewer prophets (who usually diagnose possession) in the diaspora churches, but prophets from the country where the church originated may pay visits to Britain from time to time. As in one case recorded in the case files of the Metropolitan Police, such pastors may move through the expatriate communities of their country, identifying witches. The well-known leader of a Nigerian Pentecostal church and witch-hunter, Helen Ukpabio, made more than one planned visit to London[18] in 2013, specifically to cleanse it of witches.

In Britain, children who were accused often showed some disability as well as displaying signs of distress and neglect. Among the cases from the Metropolitan Police files that I studied, nearly half showed one of a range of disabilities – physical, mental and emotional. Some children were also described as showing 'difficult behaviour', including being rebellious, disobedient or overly independent. Three, however, were described as 'exceptionally bright' and this may have been the reason they were difficult to control. Added to that, the households of immigrants, even those who have been in the U.K. for a number of years, are often under severe pressures: the adults may be waiting for papers and hence find it difficult to get jobs. The promise of migration may not have been fulfilled: expenses can be higher than expected and incomes lower, so money may not be being accumulated; the lack of success or the occurrence of illness add to the likelihood of a magical cause being sought. In addition, they are likely to be living in the least desirable neighbourhoods where everyday violence is a problem and children are regularly served with restriction orders because of their behaviour. These are all factors undermining good relations between parents and children, both at home and as migrants.

Anthropological Explanation

The problem of explaining beliefs in witchcraft has been central to the anthropological endeavour for more than half a century. During that time, anthropologists have established that beliefs in witchcraft provide explanations for the uneven distribution of health, prosperity and good fortune and have tied these beliefs to the nature of social relationships, in particular the known and common propensity of human beings to suffer envy and jealousy of those more fortunate. Beliefs are activated within the context of human lives, both by those who hope to improve their circumstances and by those with an interest in proving their power to make this happen. Individual circumstances are involved in transforming these general beliefs into specific accusations against named individuals. In the cities of Western Europe African migrants struggle to explain why they have not got their residence permits when others have; why they fail to land the good jobs that are available despite their best endeavours; why their children behave badly and show no traditional respect for their elders. When the high expectations with which they came, expecting a land of milk and honey, are not fulfilled then some Africans look for a witch to blame. The nearest and often the easiest target is presented by their children.

Some anthropologists have studied religious movements of witch-finders in Africa that occurred during the 1930s and 1940s (Richards 1935; Willis 1968; Redmayne 1970), although they were rather few. More recently the interest of the present generation of scholars (Comaroff and Comaroff 1993; Geschiere 1980) has been attracted by the outbreak of witch-hunting in many parts of Africa (Ralushai 1996). They have identified a variety of causes for the phenomenon from system change to the effects of colonialism to globalization and religious change; from Pentecostalism to the entrepreneurial activities of pastors of Independent African Churches to the breakdown of traditional institutions. Yet most of them, with very few exceptions (de Boeck and Plissart 2004; Meyer 1999), have described the accused as adults or at most adolescents.

That those accused of witchcraft should be children, rather than adults,[19] is a marked change that was could not be adequately explained by the classic anthropological theories of African witchcraft. This recent phenomenon was both described and explained by de Boeck's work in Kinshasa, in which the numbers of those accused and their fate was vividly presented. Subsequently Pereira has reported on a similar situation in northern Angola, whose peoples are of the same linguistic and cultural group as people in the adjacent Democratic Republic of the Congo. The pattern there seems very similar in both places, and indeed resembles that of accusations in the delta region of Nigeria. By studying the situation in the African diaspora, where some of the social features that de Boeck includes as explanatory factors also exist but others are missing, we can hope to refine the explanation further.

A significant feature of Pentecostalism, originally spread by European and American missionaries, as already noted, is their adherence to the doctrine of Original Sin. This belief considers children to be inherently evil, needing strict discipline and training from parents who must not be indulgent or too forgiving. It may also render children particularly liable to possession by evil spirits. The culture of colonialists from Europe has been little studied, but their support of an education system that removes children from traditional domestic labour to segregate them in schools where what they learn may distance them from parental influence, must be seen as another influence on African views of children, together with the circumstances, listed earlier, that have forced some children to learn independence at an early age and to change adult views of childhood. These are all factors that may be contributing to the designation of children as witches, but some have received less attention than others. More research on the changing views of children in Africa is clearly necessary.

Notes

Updated and reprinted by permission of the Publishers from 'Child Witches in London: Tradition and Change in Religious Practice and Belief', in *The Devil's Children: From Spirit Possession to Witchcraft, New Allegations that Affect Children*, ed. Jean La Fontaine (Farnham: Ashgate, 2009), pp. 117–128. Copyright © 2009.

1 The case was widely reported in the press. This account has been taken from *The Guardian*, 4 June 2005.
2 As Stobart (2006) reports, the use of chilli pepper as punishment need not in itself entail beliefs that the child is a witch. Here it seems to have been ancillary to other physical means of exorcism.
3 Pentecostals use the term 'deliverance' rather than the older 'exorcism'.
4 This is an edited and updated version of the article published in La Fontaine 2009.
5 This information came from an informant who had spoken to the grandparents but who wished to remain anonymous.
6 Luena Pereira tells me that she has found information that children believed to be witches were sold into slavery in the Kongo region during the nineteenth century (Luena Pereira personal communication). That is the only indication I have other than the article by Robert Brain (1970) discussed later that children were ever believed to be witches in the past. Certainly when I lived in Kinshasa from 1961 to 1963 there was no mention of children who were witches, although witchcraft was talked about (La Fontaine 1970: 184–87).
7 Similar beliefs, about children with spiritual gifts and those with spirit doubles, sometimes seen as a twin who had died, are common in West Africa. These children are thought to yearn to return to the spirit world and must be placated or they will die in order to do so.

8   According to Geschiere, this must be seen as a complaint that their food was not good enough rather than a demand for more meat as such. Chiefs, rich men and honoured visitors were distinguished by the richness of their diet, with meat often and in quantity. This complaint might then be read as one against neglect and poor treatment.

9   The nature of the boys' complaint and the fact that it was the father of one of them who fell ill, seems to me to indicate rebellion against parental authority not the authority of the elders as such. Moreover *dambe*, the new witchcraft, was the only form of magic that could be used 'inside the house' – that is, against other family members – a further indication that the issue lay within the domestic group. Finally it was the elders who provided the magical 'cure' by engaging the services of an expert.

10   See Meyer 1999; Ellis and ter Haar 2004; Anderson 2006.

11   Note however that Dein prefers to call the evil practice sorcery or black magic, rather than witchcraft since it differs from the concept of witchcraft that is found widely in Africa. Bangladeshis apparently do not believe that harm may be done by the mere fact of malicious intentions on the part of the witch (Dein 2009: 77 fn 2).

12   West Africa seems to be the most common location, while there have been scarcely any reports from East or Central Africa.

13   This is discussed more fully in the next chapter.

14   Unpublished, but referred to by D.I. Robert Pull in a presentation at a conference organised by Inform in May 2006.

15   We do not know, though, that they have not been affected in some way prior to migration.

16   This must have been due to the police expectation that such cases would involve Congolese. Forces were told of this by the department in charge.

17   BBC News, 25 January 2007. In private, the police voiced their great frustration at this legal conclusion. It is because of such cases that AFRUCA (Africans United against Child Abuse) is calling for a new law forbidding the accusation of children of witchcraft.

18   Protests by Human Rights groups disrupted some meetings, so it is not known how many she actually addressed.

19   Filip de Boeck states that adults were also being accused in Kinshasa when he was doing his research (personal communication).

Bibliography

Aguilar Molina, J. n.d. 'The Invention of Child Witches in the Democratic Republic of Congo. Social Cleansing, Religious Commerce and the Difficulties of Being a Parent in an Urban Culture'. Report for Save the Children Fund.

Anderson, A. 2006. 'Exorcism and Conversion to African Pentecostalism', *Exchange: Journal of Missiological and Ecumenical Research* 35(1): 116–33.

Brain, R. 1970. 'Child Witches', in M. Douglas (ed.), *Witchcraft Confessions and Accusations*. London: Tavistock Press, pp. 161–82.

Comaroff, J., and J. Comaroff (eds). 1993. *Modernity and its Malcontents: Ritual and Power in Postcolonial Africa*. Chicago and London: Chicago University Press.

de Boeck, F. 2009. 'At Risk, as Risk: Abandonment and Care in a World of Spiritual Insecurity', in J. La Fontaine (ed.), *The Devil's Children: From Spirit Possession to Witchcraft, New Allegations that Affect Children*. Farnham: Ashgate.

de Boeck, F., and M.-F. Plissart. 2003. 'Geographies of Exclusion: Churches and Child Witches in Kinshasa', *Beople: a magazine about a certain Belgium*, no. 6.

———. 2004. *Kinshasa: Tales of the Invisible City*. Ludion.

Dein, S. 2009. 'The *Jinn*, Black Magic and the Evil Eye among East London Bangladeshis', in J. La Fontaine (ed.), *The Devil's Children: From Spirit Possession to Witchcraft, New Allegations that Affect Children*. Farnham: Ashgate, pp. 77–102.

ECPAT (End Child Prostitution, Child Pornography and the Trafficking of Children). 2006. 'Missing Out'. A Report on Child Trafficking in the North-East, the North-West and the West Midlands. ECPAT-UK.

Ellis, S., and G. ter Haar. 2004. *Worlds of Power: Religious Thought and Political Practice in Africa*. Hurst Series in Contemporary History. London: Hurst & Co.

Evans-Pritchard, E.E. 1937. *Witchcraft, Oracles and Magic among the Azande*. Oxford: Clarendon Press.

Foxcroft, G. 2007. Supporting Victims of Witchcraft Abuse and Street Children in Nigeria. Available at http://www.humantrafficking.org/publications/593.

Geschiere, P. 1980. 'Child Witches against the Authority of their Elders: Anthropology and History in the Analysis of Witchcraft Beliefs of the Maka (Southeastern Cameroon)', in R. Schefold, J.W. Schoorl and J. Tennekes (eds), *Man, Meaning and History*. The Hague: Verhandelingen van het koninklijt Instituut voor Taal, Land- en Volkenkunde 89, pp. 268–99.

Gold, M. 2009 'Possession and Deliverance in British Pentecostal Church' in J. La Fontaine (ed.), *The Devil's Children: From Spirit Possession to Witchcraft, New Allegations that Affect Children*. Farnham: Ashgate, pp. 61–76.

Harrington, C. 2009. 'Possession as a Sacrament: The Perspective of Wicca', in J. La Fontaine (ed.), *The Devil's Children: From Spirit Possession to Witchcraft, New Allegations that Affect Children*. Farnham: Ashgate, pp. 103–108.

Haynes, N. 2012. 'Egalitarianism and Hierarchy in Copperbelt Religious Practice: On the Social Work of Pentecostal Ritual'. Seminar paper presented at the Anthropology Department, London School of Economics.

Hoskins, R. 2006. 'Torment of Africa's "Child Witches"', *The Times*, 7 February.

La Fontaine, J. 1970. *City Politics: A Study of Leopoldville 1962–63*. Cambridge: Cambridge University Press.

———. 2009. 'Child Witches in London: Tradition and Change in Religious Practice and Belief', in J. La Fontaine (ed.), *The Devil's Children: From Spirit Possession to Witchcraft, New Allegations that Affect Children*. Farnham: Ashgate, pp. 117–28.

Meyer, B. 1999. *Translating the Devil: Religion and Modernity among the Ewe of Ghana*. Edinburgh: Edinburgh University Press.

Ralushai, N.V. 1996. 'Report of the Commission of Enquiry into Witchcraft, Violence and Ritual Murders in the Northern Province of the Republic of South Africa'. Unpublished manuscript.

Redmayne, A. 1970. 'Chikanga: An African Diviner with an International Reputation', in M. Douglas (ed.), *Witchcraft Confessions and Accusations*. London: Tavistock, pp. 103–28.

Richards, A.I. 1935. 'A Modern Movement of Witch-Finders', *Africa* 8(4): 448–61.

Schmidt, B. 2009. 'The Practice of Spirit Possession in Haitian Vodou', in J. La Fontaine (ed.), *The Devil's Children: From Spirit Possession to Witchcraft, New Allegations that Affect Children*. Farnham: Ashgate, pp. 91–102.

Stobart, E. 2006. 'Child Abuse Linked to Accusations of Possession and Witchcraft', Report 750. Research commissioned by the Department of Education and Skills. Reprinted in

J. La Fontaine (ed.). 2009. *The Devil's Children: From Spirit Possession to Witchcraft, New Allegations that Affect Children*. Farnham: Ashgate, pp. 151–72.

Willis, R. 1968. 'Kamcape: An Anti-Sorcery Movement in South-West Tanzania', *Africa* 38(1): 1–15.

Chapter 6

EVIL AND CHILDREN
The Morality of Childhood

'A view of the world incorporates a view of the nature of childhood' (Cunningham 1995: 2). What human nature 'is' includes an understanding of human development, assuming a necessary development from child to adult. All human maturation entails not merely physical changes in the organism, but a process of emotional and mental change. The idea of a process of maturation itself serves to create a distinction between child and adult as the beginning and end points of it. When and how the end of the process is reached may be marked in different ways and the nature of the changes recognised differently by different societies. In all of them the final product is an adult regarded as capable of participating independently in social life; in most of them children may be regarded as unable to do so.

The moral connotations of the natural human state might be defined in quite different ways, even within one society (see Jordanova 1989: 4). British children are subject to different and even quite contradictory views of their moral nature. One of them, often labelled as 'Hobbesian' from the name of the English philosopher with whom it was associated, held that children, like animals and 'savages',[1] were driven by their instincts and wants; they lacked any sense of moral principles which they had to be taught. In recent years the label 'little monkeys' might be used affectionately to and about children, although the epithet uses a reference to their amoral, animal natures. In even stronger versions, based on the Christian doctrine of original sin, children were considered weak, inherently sinful and liable to be seduced by evil, in the form of demons and spirits. Selfishness and a lack of cooperation were accepted as characteristics of children and of savages who fought each other for what they wanted; theft was characteristic of those who had not learned the nature of private property. To teach their children moral attitudes and behaviour was a major responsibility of adults. This view was probably the most usual in pre-Industrial Britain.

For children the equation with savages might have painful consequences, as did the doctrine of original sin. Punishments for failure to
behave as adults demanded they should do might be severe. Beating children for lack of diligence in their work or study, or for breaking the rules
they were being taught, was a standard punishment,[2] while locking children up, or depriving them of food were also used as means of instilling
proper behaviour into them. In past centuries, beating was considered
good for children as it instilled morality into them, and parents who did
this by chastising them were not only teaching their children not to sin,
they were saving their souls. Protestant parents were particularly strict,
emphasising that a child's will must be broken to save its soul and rear a
'pious, disciplined, obedient and teachable child' (Ozment 1983, cited in
Cunningham 1995: 56). A common phrase referred to 'beating the devil'
out of children, and together with the epithet 'limbs of Satan' implied an
inherent association with evil.

A more positive understanding of children began to be popularised in
the late nineteenth and the twentieth centuries. The philosopher Rousseau
denied that children were evil from birth; on the contrary, he painted a
picture of undefiled innocents needing nurture and protection from the
corrupt world in which they would grow up. Ignorant they might be, but
by nature they were good, until corrupted by the evil adult world, from
which they were in danger because of their weakness and susceptibility to
harm, both physical and moral.

Rousseau went on to devise a system of education that might prevent the loss of this original innocence.[3] Books of advice on parenting
popularised these views and encouraged their adoption. This later view
emphasised the child's need for protection. If a young child is innocent
and pure at birth, only at risk of corruption and contamination by the
evils of adult society, as Rousseau claimed, then it is the responsibility
of its parents to shield it as far as possible from them. The idea of a
separate existence, of childhood as a world apart, gradually developed
from this perception of children's need to be kept away from adults.
Among the better-off this entailed a separate nursery where children
would be visited by their parents; it was the lack of such segregation
that was sometimes deemed one cause of the immorality of children in
poor households.

The idea of children as innocent victims of the evil adult world, a concept diametrically opposed to the traditional one of children as tools of
the Devil, gradually spread to become, by the early twentieth century,
the one most commonly and publicly acknowledged. By 1966, Boas
argued that the idea of children constituted a powerful cultural symbol
of purity (G. Boas 1966: 42–45), and there was ample evidence for this

view. Moreover, it was supported by news items showing that children's sufferings in the adult world of disaster and deprivation were worse than those of any adult victims. In the twenty-first century, a commercial version of this idea animates the advertisements for charity that use pictures of young children to solicit donations, rightly assuming that those who see it will be more inclined to give money to help. Less dramatically, the innocence of children also underlies the more controversial conviction that children do not lie – and so what they say, no matter how unlikely, must be relied on as truthful. This was the slogan of those who believed in the existence of satanic abuse in the 1990s (see Chapter 3).[4]

During the nineteenth and twentieth centuries the state began to provide progressively more protection for children. Universal education, which closeted children away in the world of school, and the prohibition of child labour which kept them out of work, were powerful factors in fencing in children's separate existence.[5] The implicit trust in parents' ability to ensure their children's safety began to be eroded. An important component of the horror of the alleged physical and sexual abuse of children, and the later belief in their abuse in satanic rituals, was that their parents might be complicit in their victimisation.

In Britain today there is probably no national agreement on the nature of childhood or of children (Ribbens 1994; see also Jenks 1982: 1). The consensus among social scientists seems to be that the modern view of the child owes most to Rousseau (cf. Jenks 1994) but it is clear that the more pessimistic view of human nature has not disappeared (La Fontaine 1998b). A weaker version of the negative view of childhood, the willingness to attribute to children a propensity to lie to get adults into trouble, was sufficiently common for the authors of a standard [legal] textbook[6] on children as witnesses (Spencer and Flin 1992: 318–33) to need to refute it. Shortly before that, some staff of the Department of Education opposed the introduction of telephone helplines into boarding schools, believing that children using them would try to get their teachers into trouble by telling lies about them to their parents.[7] Individual children, who commit serious crimes such as murder, are still very easily seen as evil by nature and unable to be anything other than evil.[8] Such children were spoken of as 'monsters'; it was almost as if they were not children at all, and to think of them as 'monsters' was to protect the image of all other children as naturally good.

In a study of mothers and their children at the end of the twentieth century, Ribbens recorded three different descriptive labels for children: 'little devils', 'little angels' and 'little people'. Very different judgements of children's nature are implied in these terms. The existence of such varied opinions reflects the fact that historical changes took time to spread throughout the different social classes and to permeate remote localities in the country, so that now both old and new ideas exist together. In the case of Britain, economic changes and the development of state control of education and welfare entrenched a view of childhood as a distinct mode of being (Cunningham 1995), and have altered relationships between parents and children. Where the traditional view persists, it is in a weaker form. Modern British law proscribes corporal punishment of children except as parental chastisement, which must only be of an appropriate severity ('smacking' rather than 'beating'); and there is a strong movement, led by the NSPCC, for it to be forbidden altogether.

An unexpected consequence of the protective view of childhood that accompanied the view of children as 'little angels' was that they disappeared from sight. Enclosed in the safety of nursery and school they were gradually excluded from the adult world. While representing pre-social human nature in its pure form, real children were virtually invisible (La Fontaine and Rydstrom 1998), and surprisingly little was known about their development until the middle of the twentieth century. In anthropology more attention was paid to the processes by which children were changed into adults, to 'socialisation' or 'enculturation', than to children themselves, with a few notable exceptions. Children were, so to speak, protected out of sight.

As has often been noted,[9] children were not themselves the object of much scholarly attention until comparatively recently. The idea of children as 'little people', that is as individuals, is of similarly recent origin. The scholarly interest in studying children, using observation and experiment, that developed in the second half of the twentieth century introduced a new understanding of children's development that, unlike the earlier versions, carried little moral connotation. Research on children's development has shown how children's own actions and their interaction with adults are very important elements in their growth. The most recent parenting manuals emphasise the view that children are not taught their culture or moulded into citizens by their parents and other adults alone. Social relations with their peers and outside 'the family circle' contribute to their maturation, although adults both instruct and influence. The concept of childhood implied here has been assisted into being by a later international emphasis on human rights as including children, who have been given the protection of international law. While the laws may be said to perpetuate the notion of protecting children, as the weakest members of society, they also enshrine the notion that they are individuals with rights. The view of children as individuals is still very much a minority approach however, and to many adults the idea of children having rights may seem to undermine and damage parental authority.

The revival of fundamentalist Christianity has entailed the return and spread of traditional views of children as 'wicked from birth'. The Protestant practices of the past were particularly harsh, and the twenty-first century's new Evangelical, Pentecostal and charismatic Christians resemble them closely. Professor Philip Greven has claimed that '[t]he most enduring and influential source for the widespread practice of physical punishment, both in this country and abroad, has been the Bible' (Greven 2005: 6). Janet Heimlich (2011) has documented many cases of the abuse of children resulting from the religious beliefs of their parents and the church to which they belonged. She quotes a Christian parenting expert, who, referring to the tradition of original sin, stated: 'Grandma knew that every child came into the world bearing a nature that was already corrupt, depraved; that each and every child was a natural-born criminal; and that to steer the little criminal in a prosocial direction required a combination of powerful love and powerful discipline (Rosemond 2007). The Christian psychologist James Dobson describes pain as 'a marvellous purifier' for the child (cited in Heimlich 2011: 103). These quotations contain the two most significant elements of the Christian doctrines[10] that affect the definition of children and childhood: original sin and the importance of physical punishment in changing their natural state for the better. It is thus not surprising that, while physical punishment is still strongly disapproved in Britain, a national survey undertaken for the Churches Child Protection Advisory Service reported: 'The evangelicals obviously feel concerned about the issue of smacking [corporal punishment] and are much more strongly in favour of it than non-evangelicals' (Christian Research 2006).

Concepts of children's natures saw further changes in the late twentieth century. By that time a division between older children and younger ones was reflected in different perceptions of what had become two stages of childhood: childhood proper and 'adolescence'. The use of the terms 'teenager' or 'adolescent' for older children marks a distinction that has become increasingly important, and allows both positive and negative concepts of childhood to be accepted. While young children remain the picture of innocence, the popular views of adolescence may be much more negative. The dramatic rise in the numbers of young people in the inner cities who carry knives and who belong to street gangs, some of whose members have been found guilty of murders, has caused public disquiet. Possible causes such as social factors and poor parenting have been largely ignored. The adolescents may be written of as though 'naturally wicked', and not merely products of a harsh unsympathetic environment. The influence of the media ensures that the negative view receives most attention, and hence both confirms and reinforces the stereotype.

The achievements of many young people are seemingly not enough to counteract this picture of a possible development from early childhood into delinquent adolescence. Parents may be castigated for their failure where their children 'run wild', evoking, perhaps, the earlier notion of an animal nature that has not been controlled.[11]

Finally, in a multicultural society, there are views of children that are influenced by the traditions of other cultures. To many parents who are, or whose parents were, immigrants from non-Western countries, teenagers in Britain are a fearful illustration of the dangers of the British way of bringing up children, allowing them to be undisciplined, take drugs and become the cause of disorder on the streets. A common perception is that their behaviour is the result of a lack of adequate physical punishment in their earlier years. Their own concepts of children and their upbringing may be foreign to the wider society, or seem to be at first appearance, although as will be seen, they have many elements in common with the traditional, harsher British concepts. Most of these concepts of childhood, like those of their hosts, imply a view of children as malleable, with adulthood attained through the assimilation of parental teaching and example as they grow physically. That this view is a cultural one, rather than an observation of the world around them, can be seen from the fact that there are peoples, such as the Fulani of Burkina Faso, who consider children's natures as given at birth and unaltered during maturation (La Fontaine 1999; Reisman 1990).

Many immigrants hold yet another concept of childhood that associates children directly with evil. Some of their children may be stigmatised as witches. They are believed to be inhabited by evil spirits who have taken over their bodies to use them as instruments of evil, and who endow them with the power and the will to use witchcraft to harm others. It is the possessing spirit that is evil rather than the child, but for the duration of the possession the spirit 'is' the child. So beating the child's body and causing it to suffer in various ways is considered an attack on the spirit or on Satan himself, not on the child, whose body is merely the spirit's instrument. These ideas are shared by white Pentecostalists across the Western world; they are not exclusive to those who migrate to it.

Children who are accused of being witches resemble the individuals, like child murderers, who are evil because they are not normal children. As Chapter 7 points out, children accused of witchcraft are distinguished among their peers by their abnormal behaviour. The evil, however, is perceived as entering the child from outside; unlike the orthodox Protestant view of original sin it is not considered an integral part of the child's nature. However, like Western Pentecostals, they hold the Devil and his evil servants responsible. It is thus possible for the traditional view of children as weak and ignorant, needing training to become adult to continue, though traditionally, these children would have reached adulthood earlier than their modern Western counterparts. But intractable children, often described as 'stubborn', are now liable to be accused of witchcraft whereas in the past they would have been considered weaker in mind and body than adults, and thus incapable of it.

These views are modern and, like concepts of childhood in Britain, reflect many changes in social and economic life. In Africa[12] the power of adults came, traditionally, from a number of features that were absent among children, in addition to the physical size and strength that is a universal feature of physical maturity. Maturity is defined socially in all societies, and in many African societies this might be delayed for various reasons. The kinship system ensured that children were subordinate to their parents and other senior relatives until they themselves were parents or, in some cases, until the death of all their seniors. Given the extended nature of the kinship system, this might delay social maturity until long after physical maturity. The Tallensi of northern Ghana regarded the state of having a father still alive as relegating a man to relative nonentity among his peers (Fortes 1959). In Uganda, a Gisu youth might be considered a man once he was circumcised, no matter how old he was, but he depended on his father for the permission and the necessary material goods to accomplish this transition, which the senior man could delay. Throughout Africa, girls rarely achieved independence since women were subordinate to a man all their lives, although a small measure of independence might be held by elderly widows who had not remarried, and in some societies rank allowed individual older women to achieve a status not achieved by others.

Property in all its forms was owned and controlled by adults, and hence children were dependent on adults for their basic needs. Lack of property and economic dependence thus defined children relative to adults. In many such societies wealth in herds or land was the source of political power and authority; children had neither, so they lacked the basic means to power. Even royal children were dependent until maturity and they suffered a further disadvantage as potential rivals to the ruler. Hence they might be exiled or even killed if they seemed to be the focus of revolt or disaffection (see Richards 1960: 47).

Traditional knowledge too was in the hands of adults and was acquired as much by experience as by teaching. While this was true of all everyday skills that were learned by practising them, it particularly held for spiritual powers that might depend on a long apprenticeship to an expert before they might be exercised. Young people could be regarded as ignorant into their young adulthood and beyond.

Revolutionary changes in the position of children have followed rapid social, economic and political changes in Africa. These have undermined the main sources of adult power. Filip de Boeck (2010), who was the first to report on the phenomenon of child witches in Kinshasa, the capital of the Democratic Republic of Congo, has argued that long periods of civil war, the displacement of refugees and decimation of the adult population by the AIDS epidemic had left many children without parental care and support. But they appeared to survive, demonstrating a self-sufficiency that had not been a part of the traditional image of childhood. The visible presence of children who scrape a living on the streets as prostitutes, beggars and thieves has changed the popular view of children as weak and unable to survive without adult support. That their survival depended on illegal and immoral activities encouraged adverse views of children's powers. In addition, the experience of child soldiers or of children who survived working in the Angolan diamond mines and returned with more money than many adults further undermined the superiority of adults. Western education endowed children with greater knowledge in the Western sense and thus weakened the authority parents might exercise. The erosion of the sources of parental power that supported this authority might well have encouraged parents to rely on the remaining means of asserting their authority – violence.

Similar changes in other parts of Africa, and the widespread phenomenon of children living alone in the street, damaged the perceived status of adults vis-à-vis children and has also encouraged a more negative view of children, as well as one that has credited them with more independence and evil spiritual powers. That many survived the AIDS epidemics while adults died might be interpreted as the latter's ability and will to kill using witchcraft.[13]

The new view of children in Africa differed from that originally found in the West since it stigmatised only those children who were different from 'normal' children. However the rise of Pentecostalism in Africa, following extensive missionary activities (Coleman 2000; Meyer 2004), added the final element that spread the belief in children's witchcraft. Fundamentalist Christianity, using the Bible as their source for this doctrine, declared all children were weak and sinful, an easy prey for demons and devils who might possess them and, by endowing them with the powers of witchcraft, use them as tools for Satan's purposes. Pastors in some Pentecostal churches added divination of witchcraft to their powers and might single out and accuse children in their congregations in support of what they preached about possession by evil spirits (see Conclusion). The modern African view of children has accompanied African migrants to Britain and other parts of the Western world where their pastors continue to preach against demons and witches, and identify children as practising evil. The indigenous Pentecostal and fundamentalist churches in Britain also believe in possession by devils, the servants of Satan, as do some Muslims, who may characterise a 'difficult' child as possessed of a devil. However, this does not lead Muslims to believe that children can be witches and harm others magically, a belief that is found particularly in certain African independent Christian churches.[14]

The historian Hugh Cunningham points out that one must distinguish between a concept of childhood and the lives of real children, and of course no anthropologist would dispute this, but they are not entirely distinct. Concepts of childhood held in society at large influence, though they do not entirely determine, general attitudes towards and treatment of real children, not to speak of the aims of their parents. It is thus important to consider the patterns of behaviour associated with the abstract concepts. Fundamentalist churches believe it is their mission to fight evil so that identification of possession by a demon must lead to action against it. This action, exorcism, aims to ensure that the evil spirit leaves the child's body either voluntarily or as the result of the use of force. It is traditionally used against possession by many religions. Among modern Pentecostals the treatment of children believed to be possessed of a devil is a stark demonstration of how concepts of the nature of childhood can authorise violent action against particular children.

While the commonest form of exorcism among Muslims and Christians seems to be prayer, either by the exorcising pastor or a group of the congregation; beating may also be used by Christians and Muslims alike. Not all exorcisms are carried out by a religious authority; some are carried out at home by the accusing parents, which seem often to be more violent. Children accused of witchcraft may be locked up until they accept that they are possessed; they may be starved or deprived of water to purify them, or woken from sleep several times in the night to pray. Beating and other forms of assault may be used; Kristy Bamu was punched and hit with an iron bar by his sister's partner. Some children may die under this treatment, as Kristy did. There have been few such deaths reported in Britain but many more in the United States, most of them in white families. In Africa, children may be thrown out of home to recover from their injuries or die on the street. Although the exact number of children in Africa killed during exorcism is unknown, almost certainly many more 'child witches' have died in Africa than in all Western countries together.

That the treatment of children believed to be possessed of a demon should be cruelly abusive may not seem surprising, when the perpetrators assert that it is the pain that drives the devil out and will save the children's souls. Theory and action are consistent in these instances, however damaging to children it may be. It is more difficult to explain why those children who were claimed to be innocent victims of evil persons may also be subjected to treatment which may be quite harsh. In such cases, while the children may be said to be innocents who must be believed, the actions of their supporters may imply otherwise. Although they were not beaten or starved, children believed to have been the victims of devil-worshipping Satanists were often put under severe pressure to tell what adults thought they knew.[15] To the outside world these adults, social workers, care workers in children's homes, foster parents and other believers in ritual abuse claimed to be merely mouthpieces for the children who confided in them; it was implied that they did so freely and of their own choice. The daily records kept by foster mothers who also encouraged the children to tell 'their stories' were referred to as 'the children's diaries'. One foster mother recorded in her diary that 'G. (her foster child) needed to talk tonight as the last few nights have been really restless for him. Sleep walking and he seems really frightened'. She then asked him a number of questions, encouraging his siblings to prompt him with the acceptable replies. Some children were subjected to long and frequent interviews, summaries of which were later disseminated as 'what the children said'.

'Telling' was widely seen by social workers, child psychotherapists and foster parents as therapeutic, so that putting pressure on the children was not seen as abusive or as coercion but as an essential means, not merely to discover the truth of what had happened to them, or to obtain evidence to use against the perpetrators, but to enable the children to heal and recover from their traumatic experiences. A surprising parallel is to be found in some exorcists' practices to remove evil spirits. It may be believed that for child to be exorcised they must first admit that they are possessed and are witches and only then can they be purified and the evil spirits exorcised. Some children were subjected to intensive pressure and even beatings to induce them to 'confess' as the necessary condition for exorcism. Children who denied that they were victimised in a satanic ritual, or who said they had nothing to tell, were not believed. Other elements of the beliefs in the satanic conspiracy were drawn on to explain the failure to talk. Satanists, like evil spirits, servants of Satan were believed to be controlling the child. Thus whether children were seen as inherently innocent or as sinful by nature, when certain behaviour was required of them they were equally subjected to the superior power of the adults who were in a position of authority over them.

The similarity in behaviour that has been remarked on here reminds us that spiritual beliefs exist as part of a complex whole of ideas held in any particular society. Some may be subject to greater variation than others, according to their scale and complexity; others may seem relatively uniform across society. This chapter started by focusing on the different concepts of childhood and children found in twenty-first-century Britain. These concepts may be directly opposing angels to devils, or be distinguished as religious in origin, or as secular and owing more to science. The association of these beliefs with categories of people defined by their membership in (religious) organisations or their background in ethnic cultures may be thought to explain their variation. But, as we have seen, there are other factors to take into consideration such as the relative positions of adults and children, and their relations to one another. Nor do these explanations predict with any accuracy the particular views held by individuals. There are non-believers in every category.

A further conclusion concerns the relations between beliefs and behaviour. Beliefs, even those concerning fundamental moral truths, and the actions of individuals are not directly related as cause and effect. At the end of the millennium in Britain, many more people believed that cults of Satanists were conspiring to abuse children than ever questioned an alleged victim of the cults. Among those believers who did try to obtain 'their stories' from children, the nature of the questioning and the degree of pressure used varied considerably. Some individuals who questioned children who were alleged victims might not actually have believed in the existence of the satanic conspiracies. But there are similarities between the behaviour of those questioning the alleged victims of satanic abuse and those seeking children's confessions of witchcraft that might not be expected from such different moral systems and beliefs.

Where adults had to deal with children they believed were either witches or the victims of satanic abuse, they knew what they expected them to say. Children who refused to comply with what was expected of them were subjected to physical coercion in various forms. The comparison makes clear that the reality of children's relations with adults is influenced by the power of adults relative to children as well as by general social constructs or more abstract beliefs in good or evil. For a full understanding, the behaviour of those involved is as important as concepts or theories held by the actors. The difference between what may be generally believed and the tenor of the actions individuals undertake may be as, or more, informative than an analysis of either concept or theory. Where adults' aims concern identifying and combating the forces of evil, the weakness of children makes them vulnerable to these purposes. The contrasting moral systems that have been compared here do not, of themselves, ensure different treatment of children. The context in which they determine behaviour is an essential element.

Notes

1 The parallel drawn between members of 'primitive' societies and children played an important part in the nineteenth-century theory of Human Evolution, although as far as real children were concerned that view was soon to be out of date.

2 Cunningham argues that actual parents might not treat their children as harshly as the literature implies, but there is no doubt that children were often beaten, even if the parents might be distressed at the need to do so.

3 He expounded it in a novel, *Emile*, published in 1762, for which he aroused a great deal of animosity, both individual and official.

4 This idea may also be the origin of the claim that 'recovered memories', ostensibly the psychotherapeutically assisted recall of childhood memories in adulthood, are also undeniably and invariably truthful.

5 Dr Rita Cruise O'Brien pointed out to me that in poor rural areas children's 'help' was often essential to the family economy, so sending children to school was a financial sacrifice, though they might be expected to help after school.

6 Citations refer to the second edition.

7 I evaluated a helpline for boarding schools that had been set up by ChildLine for the Department of Education in 1991. Evidence that children went to great lengths to conceal the identity of their school and the people they complained of had much less effect on the fears of members of the department than expected.

8 In 2013 the mother of Jamie Bulger, who had been killed twenty years earlier by two children when he was a toddler, was reported as asserting that they should not have been released after serving seven years of their sentence but should have been locked up 'for ever' (BBC News, 11 February 2013).

9 Aries' classic *Centuries of Childhood*, published in 1960, was the original stimulus for an examination of childhood and changes in the notion over time. See too, Hugh Cunningham 1995.

10 I have not read a quotation of Jesus' dictum that children are the basis of the Kingdom of Heaven.

11 The failures of care homes and foster parents, for which there is a good deal of evidence, are far less widely criticised.

12 In the past the power of adults in Europe depended on similar factors but the imbalance has been observed in Africa.

13 Personal communication from Prof. Sandra Wallman who told me of the findings of Eleanor Hutchinson working in Zambia, who told her that children who survived when both parents died were not uncommonly thought to have killed them by witchcraft or evil magic.

14 These are initiated by Africans and are not affiliated to the established branches of Christianity. See Conclusion.

15 See La Fontaine 1998a, Ch. 7, for a fuller account.

Bibliography

Aries, P. 1960. *Centuries of Childhood*. Harmondsworth: Penguin.

Boas, G. 1966. *The Cult of Childhood*. London: Warburg Institute.

Christian Research. 2006. 'Churches, Children and Child Protection'. Churches' Child Protection Advisory Service.

Coleman, S. 2000. *The Globalisation of Charismatic Christianity: Spreading the Gospel of Prosperity*. Cambridge: Cambridge University Press.

Cunningham, H. 1995. *Children and Childhood in Western Society since 1500*. Harlow, Essex: Longman.

de Boeck F. de. 2009. 'At Risk, as Risk: Abandonment and Care in a World of Spiritual Insecurity', in J. La Fontaine (ed.), *The Devil's Children: From Spirit Possession to Witchcraft, New Allegations that Affect Children*. Farnham: Ashcroft, pp. 129–50.

Dobson, J. 1976. *Dare to Discipline: A Psychologist Offers Urgent Advice to Parents and Teachers*. New York: Bantam Books.

Fortes, M. 1959. *Oedipus and Job in West African Religion*. Cambridge: Cambridge University Press.

Greven, P. 2005. *Spare the Child: The Religious Roots of Punishment and the Psychological Impact of Physical Abuse*. Salem Press USA.

Heimlich, J. 2011. *Breaking Their Will: Shedding Light on Religious Child Maltreatment*. Amherst, NY: Prometheus Books.

Jenks, C. (ed.). 1982. *The Sociology of Childhood: Essential Readings*. Batsford.

———. 1994. 'Child Abuse in the Postmodern Context', *Childhood* 2(3).

Jordanova, L. 1989. 'Children in History', in G. Scarfe (ed.), *Children, Parents and Politics*. Cambridge: Cambridge University Press

La Fontaine, J.S. 1998a. *Speak of the Devil: Tales of Satanic Abuse in Contemporary Britain*. Cambridge: Cambridge University Press.

———. 1998b. 'Are Children People?' in J. La Fontaine and H. Rydstrom, *The Invisibility of Children*. Linkoping, Sweden: Linkoping University, pp. 13–23.

——— (ed.). 2009. *The Devil's Children: From Spirit Possession to Witchcraft, New Allegations that Affect Children*. Farnham: Ashcroft.

La Fontaine, J.S., and H. Rydstrom. 1998. *The Invisibility of Children*. Linkoping, Sweden: Linkoping University.

Meyer, B. 2004. 'Christianity in Africa: From African Independent to Pentecostal-Charismatic Churches', *Annual Review of Anthropology* 33: 447–74.

Ozment, S. 1983. *When Fathers Ruled: Family Life in Reformation Europe*. Cambridge, MA and London: Harvard University Press.

Reisman, P. 1990. 'The Formation of Personality in Fulani Ethnopsychiatry', in M. Jackson and I. Karp (eds), *Personhood and Agency: The Experience of Self and Other in African Cultures*. Uppsala, Sweden: Uppsala University.

Ribbens, J. 1994. *Mothers and their Children*. London: Sage.

Richards, A.I. (ed.). 1960. *East African Chiefs*. London: Faber.

Rosemond, J. 2007. *Parenting by the Book: Biblical Wisdom for Raising Your Child*. New York: Simon and Schuster.

Spencer, J., and R. Flin. 1990 (2nd ed. 1993). *The Evidence of Children; The Law and the Psychology*. London: Blackstone Press.

Chapter 7

PASTORS AND WITCHES

Anywhere in London, except in the very centre and in the most affluent areas, there are the signs: notices stuck up on shop fronts, on blanked out windows or hung as banners: Deeper Life Bible Ministries; Church of the Lord; Celestial Church of Christ; Faith Tabernacle; Mountain of Fire and Miracles. They proclaim the existence of many churches. The smaller ones may occupy empty shops and offices one or two days a week. These are what Americans call store-front churches, although some have managed to acquire a permanent building for their services. Some larger churches with their own buildings may rent out space for the services of the less well-established; there may be two or three churches renting space in one building over the weekend. The church notices offer miracles, success, power to those who become members – aims that to passers-by may seem unrealistic but that attract a congregation, however small. They are not all African churches; some are Afro-Caribbean in origin[1] and congregation, but a majority of both are Pentecostal.

The number of these churches in London is very large and almost certainly similar proliferation has taken place in other major cities in the U.K. and across Europe as well, although they are uncounted. This phenomenon is not new, although newly come to the attention of the majority of London's population. In 1999 Greg Smith counted the churches in the borough of Newham (Smith 1999). Of 181 Christian congregations the largest group was Pentecostal (72 churches – 40 per cent) with 15 independent evangelical groups, just over 8 per cent; 40 per cent of them had been founded since 1980. Altogether they accounted for nearly half of the Christian congregations,[2] and today the proportions might well be tilted further towards both these categories. More recently, a senior social worker in a neighbouring borough had the number of churches in her borough[3] counted by a colleague: in round figures it was 80. A study of churches in the Borough of Southwark by the University of Roehampton, in partnership with two Christian organizations, reported 252 new Black

Majority churches there (Rogers 2013). Others may have been virtually inoperative since many fail to become established. In considering these numbers it must be remembered that some are branches of a larger church with headquarters elsewhere, and the congregations of these churches are not all local residents.

The Pentecostal churches have diverse origins: there are churches with Latin American roots, others that are Afro-Caribbean or Brazilian, and some that are native British, although the latter are few in comparison with the others. The 'African' churches may be referred to as AICs meaning either African Independent Churches or African Initiated Churches. This label refers to the origin of the church, either as a branch of a church whose main body is in Africa or as founded by a man or woman of African origin. It does not mean that these churches are exclusively African in their membership, but there tends to be a core of members who share an ethnic origin as well as the beliefs of a particular Christian denomination. London residents will often travel long distances on Sunday to attend a particular church, either because they belonged to it in the country from which they came, or because it now contains a core of their compatriots among its members. Many include the label of 'international' in their names; as well as indicating a welcome to members of all nations, this implies branches in more than one country and, for many of the churches, global ambitions.

Pentecostal churches also vary greatly in size: some assemble merely a handful of members whereas some are very large. The bigger churches are better established; they have their own buildings, some of which are impressive in their size. A former bingo hall in South London with a seating capacity of two thousand was recently bought by one of the more successful, The Redeemed Christian Church of God. These large churches can boast many branches, not all of them in the U.K. The Mountain of Fire and Miracles lists forty branches in the U.K. and states that some branches have yet to be put on their website. Some churches in London are branches of churches founded elsewhere, particularly in West Africa.[4] Celebrity preachers make well-heralded visits to their outposts in Britain. Their appearances may fill a football stadium, drawing members of other churches to listen to them as well as their own members. As migration has increased, so the churches that cater to the migrants' religious and other needs have increased in number, size and membership.

This chapter is concerned with the Pentecostal church leaders and the heads of the AICs. The latter were mostly founded by their existing leaders, who are referred to by a variety of titles: Pastors, Prophets, Teachers, Apostles. I use the term pastor for them all, but the titles they are addressed by may vary as much as the form of the church organisation. The churches are labelled independent because they have no direct connection with the established churches of the West, although many pastors have developed contacts, both personal and for the church, with similar organisations outside Africa, particularly in the United States.

Most church founders claim a direct, personal call from God to establish a church. One, formerly a journalist, told me how he resisted the call for a long time since he wanted to continue being a journalist; others have managed to keep on with professional careers as well. For example, the website of the Mountain of Fire and Miracles describes their General Overseer and founder as 'engaged in research'. A pastor whose church attracts a large membership may establish branches in the charge of subordinate pastors under the direction of the leader; others, like the Church of Cherubim and Seraphim, are organised into a series of grades through which members may ascend (Harris 2006: 48–49). Their theology has not been taught to them by any recognised training college, for their founders claim direct messages from God through visions and dreams.[5] Some have led a schism from another church. Secessions are not infrequent and churches may also divide. The careers of their founders and leaders are believed to display the gifts God has bestowed on them; their continued growth depends on the individual pastor's ability to recruit and manage an increasing number of members.

Some AICs are themselves missionary, their members believing that Europe has become so ungodly that it is their Christian duty to bring its people back to Christ (see Olofinjana 2010: 47–52). The website of Winners Chapel, a branch of the Living Faith Church, describes how its leader received the call to go beyond the borders of Nigeria and then beyond Africa as well to proselytise. Generalisations about AICs are, however, difficult to make because, while demonstrating common features of belief and ritual, they vary quite widely in the details of their history, theology, organisation and ritual. However, most emphasise the importance of the Holy Spirit, preach the source of health and prosperity as God's blessing and practise exorcism. Indeed it has been argued that exorcism can be related to the conversions they make (Anderson 2006).

Some AICs may be known as Prosperity churches because of their emphasis on the rewards that God will make to those who show their piety. Gifts to the church through its leaders usually figure prominently in the required acts of piety. A video of one such church in Lagos showed members of the congregation throwing bundles of money at the foot of the altar to be collected in baskets and dustbins by church acolytes.[6] Coleman reports that the act of giving is believed to be a manifestation of dedication and holiness, which will ultimately be rewarded by God (Coleman

2014). Other similar churches may emphasise 'Power', meaning success and influence as well as prosperity, appealing, like Prosperity churches,[7] to those who feel they lack these things.

Pentecostal churches are supported by their members' donations. Money given by the congregation goes to the founder and pastor and requests for particular donations may also be made of the congregation. A pastor in Gilbert Deya Ministries, possibly Deya himself was shown in a television documentary asking for a 'small van'.[8] It has been noted that in many churches there is no separate account for the church, but the pastor's use of it is not queried. There is also pressure to donate. In the documentary, made in London, one pastor is shown saying 'The Devil is killing your family members' to persuade members to give more.

It is not surprising therefore that Pentecostal pastors may show in their own persons the rewards of godliness: the expensive suits of the men, the amazing dresses of their elegant spouses and their well-dressed children, their large houses and expensive cars all proclaim their receipt of what is seen as God's generosity. As I have often been told, the congregations approve of this display of their pastors' wealth. They think it shows his or her access to the power of God and an ample endowment of the Spirit, which offers proof of his claims to be a channel for prosperity and all this adds lustre to the church.[9]

Apart from what they offer their members in the future, there may be facilities provided by the church that are very valuable in the present.[10] Their regular meetings are frequent: they may have religious services two or three times during the week as well as on Sundays and these may take several hours. Most churches, big and small, provide a range of activities, varied in range, that are organised for their members. Smith records that the churches he listed 'ran at least 183 "secular" community activities, ranging from children's and pensioners' clubs, [and] a night shelter for homeless people, to employment training and advice and support for refugees' (Smith 1999). Twelve years later, the full weekly programme of the Mount of Salvation church, dictated by its pastor to my research assistant, was as follows:

Monday	Visions/Dreamers Day (at 7pm)
Tuesday	Bible Class (at 7pm)
Wednesday	Women's Prayer group; 12pm–3pm
	Pm-Brothers/young men Prayers 9pm–11pm
Thursday	Full service 7pm–10pm approx.
Friday	Mercies Day; Prayer and Marking of Foreheads with anointed oil to protect against any evil
Saturday	Choir practice with choristers 4pm

Sunday   Full Service from 12 noon onwards. Testimonies; Prophesies, interpretation of visions and dreams for those gifted to do these; singing, Drums Dancing and use of other musical instruments.

This is a particularly prayerful church; others fill the week's programme and include secular activities as well. The list of what his church undertakes given by another pastor was rather different:

Work with homeless people;
Work with Youths;
Mentoring people [this may be what others refer to as counselling/solving problems]
Nursery for ages 0–5;
Saturday School: for children aged 12–16 taught to A-level standard as well as primary school children aged 5–12 years. Subjects taught: Maths; English; Mother Tongue [in this case it was Yoruba];
Community Initiatives: helping anyone of any nationality who is in need. Help for the elderly – cleaning, washing cars, gardening etc. Young people therefore also learn how to care for the vulnerable elders.

Some activities are evening ones to allow for daytime working, but in the areas where the churches are most common, unemployment is high, so many members who run daytime activities may be unemployed. A high proportion of the active volunteers seem to be women, and the second example above shows a preponderance of activities that might be described as 'women's work'. 'Activities' cater for children and young people and also look after older people. For volunteer helpers, signing up can be a full-time commitment.

As Harris vividly describes, the earliest migrants suffered agonies of loneliness and prejudiced treatment, as well as desperate poverty (Harris 2006: 46–48). The churches also helped mitigate the painful consequences of the search for educational qualifications that had motivated them to migrate. The congregations offered support as they still do, forming little islands of solidarity in the amorphous unfriendly sea of a big city. This is no new conclusion; that the welfare of migrants may be provided by their churches has long been known.

A good deal of practical help for their members is offered by AICs as the lists of their activities have indicated. Two of them stand out today: education and what could be called social welfare. African children whose command of English is still not perfect may struggle to keep up or achieve less than their ambitious parents wish for them. Others are in schools where the teaching is poor. Hence the churches offer supplementary schooling for children, which has the additional advantage in the eyes of their parents of keeping them away from the delinquents who may be their neighbours. Migrants to Britain, even those who were in professional jobs and count among the professional middle class of their home countries, may have to live in public housing in run-down areas of English cities where the schools are not remarkable for their quality. Moreover, as parents say over and over again, the example of behaviour offered by British children may be deplorable. The difficulty of controlling their children in a rapidly changing urban environment is one of the problems that face London's residents, whether born there or not.[11]

This additional function of controlling children reflects one of the big bones of contention between British society and its members of African origin.[12] For reasons that they do not understand, beating children is frowned on in Britain and the state has powers to take children away from their parents, an extraordinary idea for Africans whose children may be regarded somewhat like property. As one African mother shouted at the police who were taking her child into protective care: 'He is my child, I can beat him if I want'. The result of this English way of bringing up their children, I have often been told, can be seen in the children who do not obey their parents and misbehave in public and in the teenagers whose behaviour is dangerously violent and criminal. African parents are often extremely worried about how their children will grow up. Extra education is one way of dealing with this problem.

Social welfare is another area where the role of pastors and elders of AICs as advisors is a central feature and is as important as education. Pastors are consulted by members of their churches on most troublesome matters, ranging from not having papers, to disciplining children and divorce. They have the immense advantage of providing privacy for troubled members of the congregation to recount their worries; they will not be the source of gossip – unlike neighbours and even members of the family. There may be a formal emphasis in the church on prosperity, spiritual warfare or the force of prayer, but this does not mean that the pastors do not deal with many more practical problems that worry members of their congregations.

Health is another area of great concern, particularly if an illness or disease appears resistant to Western medical treatment or in the eyes of the patient is not properly understood. Prayer may be believed to be the answer to all such problems. The pastor's prayers are more powerful than those of the congregation; this stems from having been called by God and, as a result, being closer to the source of divine help. The churches may serve as Citizens' Advice Bureaux with special powers. Most of them virtually advertise this fact on their website, or in the case of lesser churches, on their banners and store-fronts. Their websites ask, in proper twenty-first-century English, whether there are any 'issues' that members may wish to discuss and directs them to the time, place and sometimes even the person they should approach. The range of problems that are brought is very wide: from housing to witchcraft, from how to get papers to how to get a job.

There are several factors that predispose people to prefer consulting their pastor to making use of the provisions of the state. Most important of all is the lack of match between British provisions and African expectations. British medical services may not provide an immediate cure to all ailments, especially chronic or unusual ones and, anyway, most Africans believe in shopping around for relief of their health problems, which the NHS does not encourage. Other problems, like the failure to produce sons, may have no immediate medical solution. And almost universally, Africans believe in spiritual causes for material and physical ills whereas most British doctors and nurses do not. This is a major reason for keeping away from official organisations.[13] In Pentecostal and evangelical circles, whether home-grown or African, the hand of Satan is perceived in all problems,[14] whether medical or not, and for this the cure can only be obtained through the pastor who may be approached to identify the cause and/or to provide a remedy. Interviews conducted with the pastors of nine churches in East London,[15] and the websites of others, indicated that the belief in possession by evil spirits was general. All of those interviewed said that their church practised deliverance of those possessed by evil spirits. This list included the pastors of two branch churches of the Cherubim and Seraphim, who listed mental health problems among the cures they had effected and said they practised exorcism.[16]

It is widely thought that white people do not believe in evil spirits or witchcraft,[17] and so it is useless to ask for help from state services. I have met an NHS GP who was approached by anxious parents who thought they had a witch child, but he is Congolese by origin and unworried by such concerns. He told me that he instructed his patients to consider a long list of possible causes and only when they had exhausted these to consider witchcraft. In one or two cases social services have been implored to take a particular suspected witch child into care, but this is after they have already become involved. I have not heard of any parents approaching social services to solve a witch child problem. The known differences of belief form a barrier between African families and social services, as they do between African families and their European neighbours, who do not believe in witchcraft.

What is less often emphasised can be experienced in the chatter one can hear before and after services. People congregate after church in groups to talk and mostly use languages other than English. Maintaining the use of their language is an important unintended consequence of church membership and a significant aspect of maintaining their identity. The children of migrants grow up speaking English and sometimes do not speak their parent's original language well, or at all. They may even have to be taught it. Returning from school on London's buses, children talk in fluent English to the parent who accompanies them; the parent may reply in heavily accented English or in their own mother tongue. Another way of learning is by participating in activities conducted in the parents' language. The second church of my examples above specifically teaches what is still referred to as a mother tongue.

The activities and the use of their home language maintain identity for the core of the church's membership; the common activities encourage group cohesion and provide social welfare that may not be easily available elsewhere. The implication of this is that churches are also cultural communities, bringing together migrants from the same part of Africa. Churches do not exclude people from elsewhere and members from countries other than that of the core group can certainly be found. There are other ties: kinship, friendship, common residence and workplace that also support the community that a church membership incorporates. Whether a large international church or a small store-front one, the churches draw people together. The regular meetings at church serve to maintain connections between people who live scattered across many parts of the city.

While the services provided by churches give them the stability of communities and may attract some members, the success of an AIC is demonstrated by its growth in numbers. For this the pastor is responsible and to achieve it the pastors must 'sell' themselves to members of other churches and to the non-religious. Pastors are thus effectively in competition with one another for new members. In analysing a similar situation in the United States, Moore (1994) argues persuasively that churches adopt the strategies of the marketplace and the use of the phrase 'religious marketplace' is now common. The London evidence shows that his analysis can be applied usefully there, despite its being nearly twenty years later. First the churches provide entertainment and attract attention: their services include singing and dancing, displays of possession by the Holy Spirit, speaking in tongues and healing. People dress up for church services and the atmosphere is one of an enjoyable outing. The service she had just attended was described by a young Nigerian woman as being 'spectacular',[18] and in one case in my study a man described his wife's recruitment to a Pentecostal church as moving to 'something more exciting'. On the other hand it has been pointed out that this aspect of the services provides an opportunity for young rivals of the pastor to show by their behaviour that they too are blessed by God and could develop into leaders of dissent or schism.[19]

Churches may provide miracles of healing in the services. Sufferers may be healed in front of the congregation, by the laying on of hands or by prayer, witches may be denounced and the defeat of God's enemies made visible in deliverance. These may be promised by celebrity preachers in the advertisements for their tours. The apparent cure by a pastor of a large church in Nigeria of a man who could not walk was recorded by the BBC, whose reporter also noted that he had seen the man walking normally before the service.

The pastors themselves offer help to members of the congregation who have problems. Moore notes that the pastors and their wives present themselves as a team, which is particularly helpful in marriage counselling or in offering help from either a man or a woman to members who want to talk to someone of the same gender. As has been pointed out already, pastors also offer privacy. Above all, African pastors share the beliefs and anxieties of their congregation, providing sympathy that is based on a full understanding not only of the difficulties experienced daily but of the beliefs of their congregation. In particular they understand and believe in possession by evil spirits and in witchcraft. Indeed, as Anderson writes: '"Witchcraft" and "demons" are now virtually interchangeable and synonymous terms in African Pentecostalism' (2004: 6).

Pentecostalism is characterised by a firm belief in the power of Satan and in particular, that he sends his agents to possess human beings so as to use them to promote evil in the world. Arguably the most important service that its pastors offer is the power to deliver people from the evil spirits and the witchcraft for which they are responsible and which are causing the problems in their lives. Some churches, like the Mountain of Fire and Miracles, are particularly well known for their services in this field and may be consulted by non-members as well as members. All the Pentecostal churches, which inspired the African offshoots, are dedicated to fighting evil in the forms of Satan, and of the demons who are his servants and who possess the bodies of men, women and children and provide them with evil powers of witchcraft. The Mountain of Fire and Miracles, for example, describes itself on its website as a 'ministry where your hands are trained to wage war and your fingers to fight'.[20] The majority of the writings of its leader are concerned with the fight against evil in all its forms and with deliverance as a means to expel it.

The methods used in deliverance vary considerably, an important point that may be overlooked. The older established African churches seem mostly to rely on prayer or the healing touch delivered by the hands of a pastor or specialist healer. Churches known as Aladura because of their emphasis on the power of prayer are foremost among these. Despite the alarm and fear that may be aroused in a small child at being surrounded by loudly praying adults, such methods are not physically harmful. It must be recognised as well that the prayer sessions are usually accepted as effective treatment; they are believed to remove the demons and hence neutralise the power of witchcraft. The means to reverse the possession that has turned the child as an evil servant of Satan exist within the belief system that generated alarm in the first place. Deliverance is an important part of the whole complex of beliefs. As Anderson writes: 'There is no question but that "deliverance" is a prominent product of the African religious market' (2004: 2).

The identification of witches and their deliverance from the evil spirits that possess them are powerful factors in the success of certain pastors and their churches. Those who suspect witchcraft may approach them for identification of the witch and then later for his or her deliverance. Some hold regular deliverance services that even non-members may attend. Pastors may interrupt a service to point out a suspect witch, and few members of a congregation would dare to dispute a pastor's finding. One woman who refused to accept that her 11-year-old daughter was a witch when she was accused by a pastor was ostracised by her whole family for over six months. If a deliverance has serious consequences for the delivered, as it may when the accused is a child and suffers harm, the spiritual power of the pastors may also prevent people from acting as witnesses against them and thus protect them from the authorities.[21]

It is not uncommon for pastors to identify the cause of problems to be a child in the household who has either been possessed by spirits and/or who is a witch. In nearly half of the cases studied for this research, pastors as well as parents were the accusers of children. As the last chapter has demonstrated, children are easy targets. Since it has also been recorded that problems with children are frequently the result of migration, whether from country to town or across the considerable cultural divides between one country and another, to point to a child as the source of the family's other problems is likely to meet ready acceptance. Few children are as determined as the young brothers in one Congolese family[22] who continued to deny their witchcraft through many beatings and their removal into care. The child's witchcraft is linked to misfortunes happening to and in the family, so that the parents who accuse one of their children are not only trying to rid themselves of a witch but to repair the damage that they think the witch has done.

If deliverance is a service offered to members of the congregation and a means to recruit more members for it, it is also a source of income. As well as enhancing the reputations of the pastor and the church, deliverances enrich them. Pastors usually charge a fee[23] for evaluating a suspicion of witchcraft, and if the allegation is confirmed, which it usually is, then a further fee must be paid for the deliverance. While the fees are said to be high relative to the earnings of most parents, it was not possible to get a figure for their charges from pastors or their ministries. Pastor James from Gilbert Deya Ministries who figured in the Channel 4 programme already cited, at first demanded £1,000 to deliver a young woman [an undercover reporter] but accepted £170, giving her participation in a group deliverance, where she had to pay a further fee – an undisclosed sum. Of course the more famous the pastor and the better publicised his success in deliverance, the more he can charge; but also the more likely that his church will flourish and attract many members (see also Pype 2012).

Churches offer their members an improvement in their lot in life. This has two related aspects: the first is endowing those blessed by the Holy Spirit with money, power and prestige in a demonstration of the power of the Holy Spirit (Harris 2006). Just as important is the role of deliverance in removing the obstacles and impediments to a successful life. When troubled with a problem, whether medical or spiritual, several churches may be tried to find a solution. The pastor who provides it may well earn the allegiance of the person who feels his or her distress alleviated (cf. Anderson 2004).

If the religious market place is considered as a whole, the active competitors within it are the pastors. They vie with one another for numbers of followers, for fame, and for the result of both of these: wealth. An important way to success is to make a reputation for finding witches and delivering their victims, thus solving the problems believed to be caused by witchcraft. Pastors are thereby given a significant interest in identifying many witches. Accumulating numbers of successful deliverances inevitably encourages the identification of members of the community who cannot defend themselves against accusations – that is, children. They are also more easily persuaded to 'confess' to harbouring an evil spirit. Parents whose fears for their children are exacerbated by what they see around them may be encouraged by the pastor's sermons and actions to suspect that the most difficult children are possessed by evil spirits. At a meeting of Congolese women I asked why they thought there had been a change in those accused; I told them I had lived in Kinshasa in the 1960s when there had been no child witches; what had changed? One woman replied: 'We did not know that the children were witches until the pastors told us'.

The competition between pastors in the London religious marketplace cannot help but increase the number of children who are accused of witchcraft. Anderson (2006) has shown that exorcisms lead to conversions and if, as I have argued here, parents are motivated to accept an accusation against a child by their anxiety about their upbringing, and if children are more easily persuaded than adults to accept accusations of witchcraft, then more allegations of witchcraft against children will be the result of the search for more conversions. As jobs get harder to find, the competition in the religious marketplace must increase, both because of the increase in people's problems that need solutions and as a result of the recruitment of more unemployed people who take up the role of pastor. As the competition for power in both material and spiritual forms intensifies, so will the number of accusations of witchcraft. The religious marketplace thus generates examples of the evil that the pastor and his church are battling against, producing manifest proof of the prevalence of evil. In other words, the pastors help to create the witch-children they need to deliver so as to prosper.[24]

Notes

1 I was reminded by Dr Hermione Harris that it is hard to distinguish the African ones by their names alone, however the names listed have been checked and they refer to churches with African origins. I have benefitted a great deal from conversations with her on the subject of African Independent Churches.

2 Those who declared the number of their members (166 organisations) reported average congregations of 134 (Smith 1999, appendix).

3 There are thirty-three boroughs in London together with two, historically distinct, cities: Westminster and the financial district, the City of London.

4 On the other hand, some churches have been founded in London (and probably other big European cities) and have later established branches in Africa.

5 I have been told by Silvia de Faveri that during her fieldwork in Kinshasa, DRC, she met illiterate pastors. I have never met one in London and, according to their websites, many are well-, even university-educated. The website of the Mountain of Fire and Miracles describes their founder and General Overseer as having a first class honours degree in Microbiology from the University of Lagos, Nigeria, and a Ph.D. in Molecular Genetics from the University of Reading in the U.K.; and Greg Smith refers to the leader of the United Redeemed Church as having formerly been a doctor.

6 Documentary entitled 'Nigeria's Millionaire Preachers' in Channel 4's *Unreported World* series (Episode 14), reporter Seyi Rhodes, shown on 28 October 2011.

7 For an account of the Prosperity churches, see Coleman 2014. See also Harris 2014, and for a detailed account of one such church, Harris 2006.

8 'Britain's Witch Children', shown on Channel 4's *Dispatches*, 26 July 2010.

9 Compare the well-known analysis by Ernest Gellner in *Saints of the Atlas* (1969) of the fame of holy men in Morocco. Gellner shows that although the people say that followers flock to a saint because he is famous for his holiness, in fact he is famous because people flock to him. Similarly members of Pentecostal churches may claim their pastor is rich

because God favours him, whereas an observer might conclude that he is believed to be favoured because he is rich.

10   I wrote this before coming across Allan Anderson's more elegant formulation that the churches provide 'more tangible help in this world as well as in the next' (Anderson 2004: 122).

11   Note the comment by David Martin (2002: 98) that 'loss of parental control' was one of the causes of household tensions and problems among migrants. Little has changed in the decade or so since that was published.

12   Katrin Maier, a Ph.D. anthropology student at the University of Sussex, kindly talked to me about her (then) current research in South London, and I thank her for these very interesting and useful discussions. See Maier 2012 for her completed doctoral thesis.

13   The other may be that they are afraid that their papers are not in order.

14   See the Korean Pentecostal pastor quoted in Anderson (2004) who said that 'Poverty is the curse of Satan'. For similar views in British churches, see Webster 2011.

15   Many other leaders were also approached for interviews but either ignored the request or refused it.

16   This adoption of exorcism constitutes a change since the praying (Aladura) churches did not previously believe in exorcism (Harris 2006: 125). In email correspondence, Dr Harris agreed that some churches might well have adopted the practice since finishing her fieldwork.

17   In this of course they are over-generalising, as white evangelicals also believe in evil spirits (see Gold 2009; Webster 2011).

18   In the documentary mentioned in Note 8 above.

19   Speaking of pastors in Pentecostal congregations in the Copperbelt, Naomi Haynes pointed out that, postulating the even-handedness of the Spirit, '[a]ny believer might receive a special anointing from God, and with it religious authority, potentially resulting in a schism, as believers begin to gather around him rather than the pastor they had previously followed' (Haynes n.d.: 18). I thank her for letting me see her manuscript in advance of publication.

20   www.mountainoffire.org (accessed 28 February 2013).

21   In two cases in my sample the police had what seemed to be a good case, but it fell apart when witnesses were unwilling to testify.

22   I acted as expert witness in the case of the N. children.

23   These may be considered 'donations' and can be quite large relative to the family income.

24   de Boeck has pointed out (2009: 146–1477) that the situation is a complicated one. I do not intend to give the impression that pastors consciously try to encourage accusations against children, but merely try to show the unintended consequences of their preaching and practice. There are also a few pastors who bravely oppose their colleagues' beliefs and deny the existence of witchcraft.

Bibliography

Anderson, A. 2004 *An Introduction to Pentecostalism*. Cambridge: Cambridge University Press.

————. 2006. 'Exorcism and Conversion to African Pentecostalism', Exchange: Journal of Missiological and Ecumenical Research 35(1): 116–33.

Coleman, S. 2014. 'Between Faith and Fraudulence? Sincerity and Sacrifice in Prosperity Christianity', in A. van Eck Duymaer van Twist (ed.), *Minority Religions and Fraud: In Good Faith*. Inform Series on Minority Religions and Spiritual Movements. Farnham: Ashgate, pp. 73–90.

de Boeck, F. 2009. 'At Risk, as Risk: Abandonment and Care in a World of Spiritual Insecurity', in J. La Fontaine (ed.), *The Devil's Children: From Spirit Possession to Witchcraft, New Allegations that Affect Children*. Farnham: Ashgate.

Gellner, E. 1969. *Saints of the Atlas*. London: Weidenfeld & Nicholson.

Gold, M. 2009. 'Possession and Deliverance in a British Pentecostal Church', in J. La Fontaine (ed.), *The Devil's Children: From Spirit Possession to Witchcraft, New Allegations that Affect Children*. Farnham: Ashgate, pp. 61–76.

Harris, H. 2006. *Yoruba in Diaspora: An African Church in London*. New York and Basingstoke: Palgrave Macmillan.

————. 2014. 'Sex Work and Ceremonies: The Trafficking of Young Nigerian Women into Britain', in A. van Eck Duymaer van Twist (ed.), *Minoritiy Religions and Fraud: In Good Faith*, Inform Series on Minority Religions and Spiritual Movements. Farnham: Ashgate.

Haynes, N. n.d. 'Egalitarianism and Hierarchy in Copperbelt Religious Practice: On the Social Work of Pentecostal Ritual'. Paper presented at the London School of Economics Anthropology Department.

Maier, K. 2012. 'Redeeming London: Gender, Self and Mobility among Nigerian Pentecostals'. Doctoral thesis, University of Sussex.

Martin, D. 2002. *Pentecostalism: The World Their Parish*. Oxford: Blackwells.

Moore, A. Laurence. 1994. *Selling God: American Religion in the Marketplace of Culture*. Oxford: Oxford University Press.

Olofinjana, I. 2010. *Reverse in Ministry and Missions: Africans in the Dark Continent of Europe. An Historical Study of African Churches in Europe*. Milton Keynes: AuthorHouse.

Pype, K. 2012. *The Making of the Pentecostal Melodrama: Religion, Media and Gender in Kinshasa*. New York: Berghahn Books.

Rogers, A. 2013. 'Being Built Together: A Story of New Black Majority Churches in the London Borough of Southwark'. Report of a joint project by the University of Roehampton, 'Southwark for Jesus' and 'Churches Together in South London'.

Smith, G. 1999. 'The Christ of the Barking Road; Religious Organisations in Newham in 1998–99'. Paper accompanying the 3rd Edition of Directory of Religious Groups in Newham, published by Aston Charities, London.

Van Eck Duymaer Van Twist, A. (ed.). 2014. *Minoritiy Religions and Fraud: In Good Faith*, Inform Series on Minority Religions and Spiritual Movements. Farnham: Ashgate.

Webster, J. 2011. 'The Immanence of Transcendence: God and the Devil on the Aberdeenshire Coast'. Paper given to Religion Forum, London School of Economics.

Chapter 8

LONDON'S WITCH CHILDREN

Children may be at risk from a number of different spiritual or religious beliefs that occasion their mistreatment and damage them psychologically and/or physically; of course not all of these risks have to do with witchcraft. A firm belief in the Christian doctrine of Original Sin may result in the severe physical abuse of children in the conviction that it is a means to ensure their proper moral development, as we have seen (Chapter 7). Alternatively, the fear of witches, demons or other evil spirits can be the cause of some strange behaviour, which may be reported to the authorities, but then proves to be neither illegal nor abusive of a child. In the abuse of a child, ideas of witchcraft may be closely associated with other notions, such as a belief in possession by evil spirits; in other, similar cases, only one such belief may be seen to be involved. As a result of this diversity of belief and associated action, general conclusions that are widely valid are hard to draw.

Most of the chapters in this volume discuss ideas concerning witchcraft and other forms of evil that are held either in parts of Africa or in Europe. But witchcraft is not merely a matter of belief but may have direct results in action. This chapter is concerned with the actions that resulted from beliefs in witchcraft and particularly with records of accusations made against children in England that they were witches, or were using witchcraft. Most of the known victims of these accusations were living in London. Such accusations occur elsewhere in the UK as well, though largely in the cities, since that is where the relevant[1] migrant population has mainly settled. Most of them are of African origin but children may be accused of witchcraft in other parts of the world, such as India or Papua New Guinea, but in those places they are more likely to be accused together with their mothers. What distinguishes the accusation of African children, whether in parts of Africa itself or as migrants, is that they are accused independently of their relatives, who are often the accusers.

These accusations are the product, not of any one factor but of a variety of the factors already mentioned: the concepts of human evil, a background of poverty and failure when others succeed, of former traumatic events in the homeland, of difficulties as migrants and of conflict within the household. Witchcraft and the work of evil spirits are frequently concluded to be the cause of all these misfortunes; the belief that children may harbour evil in the form of possessing spirits and may have the power to cause harm in those around them may focus animosity on the children. The combination of many different circumstances results in accusations singling out particular children. The accusations become public when actions designed to deliver the child harm him or her and some of them then involve the authorities.

We do not know what the rate of accusations in London is or how it compares with that of other cities, as research on this topic has only just started and London has been the initial focus. It is probable that fewer cases occur among the migrant communities in London than in parts of Nigeria and the Democratic Republic of Congo where large numbers of them have been reported. One pastor said that witches were so numerous in Africa they could not be eradicated, but here in London there was a chance to remove them all. The figures that are quoted for London resemble those for child abuse generally – that is, they refer to reported cases and, as for cases of child abuse, there is every reason to think that reported cases form only a small proportion of their actual incidence. The quantitative analyses below are therefore not definitive but the patterns they show support conclusions drawn from the more qualitative part of my study and are therefore of interest. The figures could be altered by a more complete and a more accurate coverage of cases, if such is ever possible.

In itself, the issue of accusations is not straightforward. It is worth noting to begin with that some people may make a joking accusation of witchcraft to friends or throw an accusation at a child in a moment of exasperation. One child explained that her stepmother only called her a witch when she was angry, implying she did not mean it. In another instance, an adult who had allegedly said a child was a witch claimed that it had been said to tease and that it was not really meant. In both of these instances the context made it possible that this was merely an excuse and not quite true. However, on another occasion, talking to a Nigerian friend about this research evoked the remark that she must be careful not to call her friends or children witches in fun any more or she might be arrested. She is not a member of a Pentecostal church and she was clearly saying this jokingly. When I asked if other people also made flippant accusations she agreed that they did.

Serious accusations may be made in private before ever they are aired in public. Even in rural villages in Uganda[2] in the 1950s, when to believe in witchcraft was the norm, it was not considered wise or seemly to talk about such things, except confidentially and in lowered voices. Some people, and this is still the belief in some communities and in certain places, thought that talking about witchcraft might attract attacks of it or lead people to believe that you might yourself be a witch, if you talked so freely about witchcraft. Rumour and gossip abounded but outright accusations were infrequent and made mostly under the influence of extreme emotions such as rage or grief. The existence of witches or witchcraft in one's family was, and is still, considered shameful and people try to keep allegations within the family circle so that neighbours do not gossip. Of course in Europe, African communities may be scattered through large conurbations, but, even so, the networks along which gossip may run are well-established and active so that caution may still be felt to be necessary. In seven instances in my research it was members of the wider kin network that were reported as accusing the child and in one other a 'friend of the family', indicating how information about suspicions may spread.

The Context of Research

Before considering the light that reported accusations may throw on witchcraft in London and the subsequent actions generated by the beliefs, the nature of the figures used in this chapter must be considered because it places some limitations on the weight we can give to the data and findings. First there is the undoubted fact that to undertake research into allegations of witchcraft in a modern city in Europe is a difficult task. London boroughs, from whom permission must be obtained before research involving children can be undertaken, have more independence than is commonly recognised. Local government and its constituent departments and officers all work to the central government regulations which establish their roles and functions. However, their attitudes and reactions to events and people are influenced by the borough in which they work and its culture, and they have control of the enforcement of the regulations that define their work. Both the formal structure and its informal working can prove extremely obstructive to anthropological research.[3]

When I applied to the Association of Directors of Children's Services for permission to undertake research, approval was given with the proviso that they were not able to ensure that the borough councils would take the same view. They did not: five out of the seven boroughs I approached, after having obtained this initial permission, still refused to authorise me to undertake the research.

The reasons for this can only be conjectured and may not always be the same as those that are given, if any, to an applicant. Of course, councils and their departments, like all organisations, maintain their boundaries by excluding people who do not belong; the power to do so is an aspect of their authority. Where London boroughs are concerned, such intruders consist largely of the public and the media. As far as members of the public are concerned, they may be seen, not as the paymasters they undoubtedly are, but as an intrusive nuisance. The media are identified as a threat, particularly to social services. It is fair to say that social services get a bad press whatever they do, so their nervousness is quite intelligible. Journalists are not always recognizable and anyone wishing to do 'research' might be a journalist in disguise who will expose their secrets and cause them to be publicly attacked. For government employees, including the police, any claim to professional ethics is irrelevant; in addition the research methods of many disciplines, of which anthropology is certainly one, may not be understood. What may be required is a legal constraint on all outsiders, such as that provided by signing the Official Secrets Act.[4] Otherwise no-one can be trusted. In this they are like the parents who may resolutely refuse to speak, in case stories about the witchcraft they are suffering are leaked to the outside world.

The difficulties of obtaining research clearance are compounded when questions come to be asked about these beliefs, largely held by immigrants,[5] by members of the host nation. It is widely acknowledged that Europeans do not understand witchcraft; worse, they do not believe in it. Thus when someone white and English asks questions about witchcraft allegations, a blank wall of denial is the usual response. When I attended a meeting of the Nigerian Women's Association I asked if anyone knew of cases where children had been thought to be witches. My question was met with silence. One woman then said that such things belonged to the past and to remote, backward communities in Africa. I was told later by a friend who had been with me that this same woman told a later meeting that was discussing my visit that she herself had been accused when a child. In a meeting of pastors, one of them declared, at the outset of my research, that he knew nothing; but later, after hearing my report on what research seemed to have shown, he was outraged. He rebuked me for daring to talk about witchcraft, saying that he was the one to talk about such matters, as only he knew all about them.

The apparent incidence of witchcraft accusations against children may be somewhat reduced by the practice of returning them to Africa to be 'treated' there. It is said to be a resort of Congolese residents in the U.K., but there is no evidence to support (or indeed refute) this notion, although it seems likely to take place in some cases. Two children to whom this had happened were identified in Kinshasa, a girl and a boy aged 10 and 13 respectively. The girl was rescued and now lives in a refuge in Kinshasa that was founded and is supported by a Congolese pastor living in London. She was reported by him to be well but wishing to return to what she considers her home: London. Her picture shows a sad face. The other, the boy, featured in a television documentary about child witches in Kinshasa. He was given the name of Londres from his birthplace and had been promised a return there, but this did not eventuate. What happened to him subsequently is not clear, although his kin have denied that he had been, or was being, ill-treated. Neither of these children were able to speak Lingala (the lingua franca of the city) when they were sent to Kinshasa, or French, the official language of the state, so their ability to survive on their own would have been severely limited. One of the children did undergo a deliverance ritual, the other did not, but it is common for such children, whether or not they have been delivered, to be rejected by their kin there and to have to live on the streets. How many children are returned to Africa in this manner and how many survive are other unknowns.

In London, and if children are concerned, adults are particularly wary of talking to the authorities. It is generally known that children are pro-tected legally and may be removed from the jurisdiction of their parents by the social services.[6] Attitudes to this are ambivalent: on the one hand, some parents may want the child they believe to be a witch to be removed into care to protect other members of the family from the possibility of harm; on the other hand, removal into care is not always considered a complete solution of the trouble, since it does not get rid of the evil spirits that may be believed to have given their child the power of witchcraft, and it may be thought that they can strike just as well from a distance. Some parents may prefer to send their children to Africa to be delivered there, which is usually a far from happy outcome for the children, even if their parents have seen it as the solution as far as they are concerned.

Children accused of witchcraft in modern European cities are easily ignored by people outside the household. The privacy afforded domestic life by the solid architecture of the houses and flats prevents neighbours from knowing as much as they would in the more open, flimsy housing of most African towns and villages. Neighbours in English cities also tend to mind their own business, as is considered proper. Where authorities are concerned, the absence of belief in witchcraft also means a tendency to dis-miss a child's story if he or she tries to tell them what is happening. Their ignorance makes it unlikely that either white neighbours or the authorities will realise how a child suspected of witchcraft may be seriously ill-treated.

Finally, and most unfortunately, the general tendency of any English adult when faced with family problems is only to talk and listen to the responsible adults. As in the case of other forms of abuse, the invisibility of children[7] has prevented them from telling about the witchcraft accusations against them. This lack of communication is compounded for children who do not speak the language of their new country. Victoria Climbié, who mainly spoke the French of Cote d'Ivoire, her home country, was seen by doctors, social workers and police, none of whom seemed to have been able to communicate with the child, or make serious efforts to do so.

In Africa, in places where children are accused of witchcraft, they are far from hidden: in towns, many if not most are thrown out of their homes to survive as best they may. They are to be seen picking up a precarious living on the streets of towns and villages in the areas particularly afflicted with an upsurge of these beliefs (de Boeck 2004). Some obtain refuge with charities or other organisations and it is they who provide the information we have on the problem in Kinshasa or the villages of the Nigerian Delta.. By contrast, when children are accused of witchcraft in Europe or North America they have usually come to public notice only when the abuse of the alleged witch has resulted in serious harm or death and the national media have been involved. Three cases, in 2000, 2005 and 2010, that were featured in the media have already been discussed (see Chapter 6). Two of the cases are included in my figures but very few of the children in the cases discussed in this chapter were the subject of widespread, or indeed any, media coverage.[8]

The figures below refer mainly to cases reported to the Metropolitan Police. Most of them were the result of a Metropolitan Police project, named Project Violet, which had been set up in 2005 in the aftermath of the case of Victoria Climbié. Project Violet aimed to specialise in cases where religious beliefs motivated the abuse of children. At its inception, Carly Thrale,[9] employed by the Metropolitan Police, was given the job of searching earlier files for relevant material. Her report was followed by Eleanor Stobart's research (2006), commissioned by the DfES. It is likely that Stobart used Thrale's collection of cases as the basis for her research as I have done. In my case, however, there was information referring to subsequent cases to add to it.

Once Project Violet had been established, cases seen as involving religious or other spiritual beliefs were marked in the computer database and so reported to the project team. They covered the period from 2005 to 2008 inclusive; the Thrale list extended the period covered back to the year 2000. A good deal of detailed information was lacking in many cases.

Project Violet did not specialise in witchcraft cases; any case that had some association with a spiritual belief was included. Since modern ideas of witchcraft may include allegations of possession by an evil spirit, I considered carefully all cases involving allegations of possession. I removed all those that clearly did not include mention of witchcraft but the remainder were included. In the end, the total number of cases was much reduced, leaving twenty-six cases clearly involving witchcraft accusations and sixteen cases of spirit possession with the possibility that witchcraft was also suspected, over a period of eight years. There were more reports in the later than the earlier years, but as the dates associated with cases were often the dates when a report was made, which might differ from the date of an accusation, I have not provided a breakdown of the years. The cases have been presented in simple tabular form; with such small numbers and no guarantee that all cases for the period were included, statistical analysis would be misleading.

Events reported to the Metropolitan Police have a 'docket', which is a short initial report, and may also have a 'file', which contains witness statements, reports of interviews and any additional information that is received. Not all dockets are followed by files, if, for example, for some reason the case is not taken further. Obviously there was more information in those cases where there were files. Some information on cases that had been reported to the police after two earlier investigations had been completed was added, as were nine cases that I discovered in my research elsewhere. Finally I included cases that were reported in the press if they were not to be found among the police files.[10]

My total number of cases concerning witchcraft accusations against children was much reduced from the numbers usually claimed. For example, in a workshop held at the London School of Economics in April 2013 members of the Project Violet team reported they dealt with nine or ten cases a year. It was not clear whether the cases reported in 2013 were only those involving witchcraft; if they were, the incidence would have meant between seventy and a hundred over the period I covered, which was very much greater than the actual number recorded. Nevertheless it is very likely that the cases used in this chapter underrepresent the actual incidence, of which we have no reliable information. It is the regularities that can be perceived that are of interest, rather than the actual numbers in the tables. With these caveats I pass on to the consideration of cases.

Origins

Where ethnicity is concerned, there was some bias in the reporting of the origins of the people involved in cases of witchcraft accusation. Large numbers of cases involving children were first recorded in Kinshasa (de Boeck

2001) and in the larger area of the Congo basin, including northern Angola (Pereira 2011). The facts were widely reported by the media, figuring in several television documentaries. During the first phase of their discovery, accusations of witchcraft against children were generally considered to be a phenomenon limited to the Democratic Republic of Congo (Thrale 2005). The media's concentration on the DRC may have been the cause of an obvious bias in reporting, which resulted in the large numbers of cases among Congolese initially reported to Project Violet – some prominent members of the Congolese expatriate community certainly thought so.[11] It is now common to find the Lingala term for witchcraft and sorcery, *kindoki*, which is used in Kinshasa and elsewhere in the DRC, used to mean all African beliefs in witchcraft. In fact beliefs vary in detail across different cultural areas and so using a term with local meanings for them all may be misleading.

The phenomenon of child witches is also very common in southern Nigeria and allegations are now reported in the eastern district of the Democratic Republic of Congo as well as across West Africa. Victoria Climbié, whose death at the hands of her accusers was the first to get extensive coverage by the press and whose case resulted in the establishment of Project Violet, was from Cote d'Ivoire. The growing literature indicates that there are similar cases in other parts of West and Central Africa, although in Ghana, as well as in Eastern and Southern Africa, the elderly, particularly elderly women, who were the victims of such accusations in the past, are still more likely to be accused in those countries.[12]

It might be expected that the reported cases involving witchcraft accusations in London would tend to come more often from parts of London where there are large African communities, such as Southwark, Lambeth and Newham, although research has shown recently that these boroughs are losing a proportion of their African populations (Paccoud 2014: 36). But most boroughs reported only a single case, although Barnet, Enfield and Hackney reported three each, and Haringey five. Variations when the figures are so small cannot be counted as statistically significant, but it is surprising that Southwark, which still has by far the largest African population of any borough, did not report any at all. The movement of African migrants to the outer London boroughs, recorded in recent research, may account for some of the unexpected figures. However, experience suggests that it is the sensitivity of the authorities to the issue and their knowledge of it that affects the rate of reporting at this stage, rather than the actual incidence of cases.

The reported countries of origin of the accused in the police cases are given below, although there were many omissions in the notes as the category 'not recorded' indicates.

Table 8.1 Country of Origin of Parents of Accused Children

Country	Witchcraft	Possession by spirits – possible witchcraft
Congo (DRC)	12[a]	6
Angola	2	2
Ghana	2	0
Nigeria	3	0
Total recorded	19	8
Not recorded	7	8
Total cases	26	16

Note: I do not distinguish between children born in the U.K. and those who came here as children, since it is the background culture that is most important.
[a] Two cases were linked, so have been counted together as one case.

As might be expected there is a preponderance of Congolese, due to the records of Project Violet and because of Carly Thrale's work. It is also worth noticing that there are no cases involving Africans from East or Central Africa. It seems that in those areas, children are still largely the victims, rather than the perpetrators, of witchcraft.[13]

The Accused Children

An accusation of witchcraft concerns a single child in almost all cases. In only five cases, whether concerning accusations of witchcraft or spirit possession, was more than one child in a family accused. In one of them, two boys aged 10 and 8 arrived in the U.K. to join parents whom they had not seen since they were very young. Indeed the younger boy was only 4 when his mother left him and his brother in Kinshasa to follow her husband to London. There were two older children with their parents, both girls, and two boys born in England, whom the accused children had never seen. None of the other children were accused of witchcraft, although one of the girls became very disturbed after her brothers were taken into care, and was finally placed in secure accommodation. Despite her condition, which might appear to satisfy the criteria for being possessed and/or being a witch, her parents did not accuse her. Her two brothers were both accused of witchcraft by their father.

Witchcraft accusations were made against a particular individual who was deemed to be the witch, and in no case was another child accused after the accused sibling(s) was/were removed into care. In some cases Social Services took all the children into care, presumably so that some other child in the family would not be accused. This possibly reflected the assumption that such an accusation is like making the child a family scapegoat. Family therapy is reputed to have used the concept of scape-goating for many years;[14] if it is true that family therapy and social work are closely connected, as has often been said, this may be why this paral-lel is readily, but wrongly, drawn when a child is accused of witchcraft. However, these cases make quite clear that a witch is not a scapegoat who will be replaced by another if removed, but an individual source of danger to the household. The only safeguard for the family is to exorcise the evil spirit possessing the identified witch. Unless several children are accused of witchcraft together at the same time, then the other children seem to be safe from accusation.

An analysis of the age and gender of the children accused does not allow one to draw firm conclusions although there are interesting sug-gestions in the data. As can be seen below, there are more girls accused of witchcraft (17) than boys (11) but more boys than girls are accused of possession by spirits (13 to 9); so if, as suggested earlier, the allegation of possession does imply a suspicion or accusation of witchcraft, then the numbers of boys and girls are more or less even. The girls seem younger, being more likely to be ten and under, while the boys, unlike the victims in Stobart's report, are mostly over 11 (see below). I was told more than once that child witches are children who are 'stubborn' – that is: disobe-dient, not tractable or willing to follow adult guidance or to learn rules of behaviour. They are the sort of children described in England as 'difficult'.

Table 8.2 Accused Children by Age and Gender

Age of witchcraft Age	Girls	Boys	Age unknown
5 & under	1	1	1
6–10	8	1	
11–15	5	8	
16+	3	1	
Total	17	11	1
Accused of possession by spirits Age	Girls	Boys	Age unknown
5 & under	0	2	
6–10	3	7	2
11–15	4	3	
16+	2		
Total	9	12	2

It may be that the ages of the children are relevant if boys and girls resist parental teaching at different ages; however, this remains to be tested by further research.

The London children who were accused of witchcraft resembled similar children in Kinshasa or in southern Nigeria. The children were usually marked out from their siblings and half-siblings in the same ways as reported for Kinshasa by de Boeck (2009). Some distinguishing marks were a matter of disability: autism was suggested in four cases and one little girl was an elective mute. Particular behaviour was also cited: it was reported in the case of Kristy Bamu that his brother-in-law was convinced he was a witch when he wet himself (though he had been unable to get into the bathroom). There were several cases in which an accused child was said to be badly behaved, self-harming or stealing. (In such cases an English child might be considered 'disturbed'.) Behaving badly at school was another reason for believing a child to be possessed or a witch, a characteristic that does not seem to figure anywhere in accounts of child witches in Africa, probably because going to school is not universal. In London what children do at school is significant, because education is generally seen as very important; in addition, a child's bad behaviour in school may result in difficulties with the teachers and embarrassment for the parents. But that is the sole cause of suspicion that reflects the fact that these are children accused in London, rather than somewhere in Africa.

The Locus of Accusations

As an obvious result of such features and, indeed, as was reported in the earliest research into the phenomenon, contemporary accusations of witchcraft are largely domestic affairs (see de Boeck 2001: 130, 2004; Stobart 2006: 158). This in itself shows changes from the traditional pattern where it was unusual to find accusations between members of a single household. The difficulties and troubles that are associated with witchcraft accusations are household ones: parents' unemployment, their failure to obtain residential status or other necessary 'papers', shortage of money, badly behaved children, sickness, divorce and death – all these represent the sort of ill fortune that do not afflict all African families in London equally and are a source of distress when they do. De Boeck has argued that poverty alone cannot account for witchcraft allegations against children and cites accusations against those in better-off households and in what he sees as the more 'relaxed' atmosphere of migrant communities (de Boeck 2009: 135). However, there is no doubt that *relative* poverty can have its effect on migrants who are unable to reach the income of the comfortably-off Londoners they see about them, and whom they came to the U.K. to emulate. In the few cases where there was any information it showed that the adults in the household were employed (if at all) in jobs below their levels of education, skills or ambition; for example, an experienced journalist was stacking boxes in a supermarket storeroom. The seeming disregard of their qualifications may be yet another source of frustration for many migrants.

This research also supports the established conclusion that children who are accused of witchcraft are not fully integrated into the household in which they live (de Boeck 2004; Stobart 2006). Few of these households in which witchcraft accusations are made against a child or children consist of a simple nuclear household of parents and their children. Only three London cases involved such a household. In all the others the composition of the household showed the effects of death, divorce and remarriage, or abandonment by the original male head. Thus the majority of the households in which witchcraft accusations are made against children are 'reconstituted' households, where the children are step-siblings or half-siblings – the offspring of former unions that have not lasted. Some children may only have a tie of kinship to one other member of the household. These households are unlikely to be typical of the communities from which they are drawn, which seem to have a solid core of stable, successful marriages; on the other hand, these more stable households are the situations where trafficked children, imported as domestic labour, are to be found, and there were some instances of this in the sample (see below).

The Accusers

As has been discussed earlier in this chapter, pastors are often involved in findings of witchcraft, and in ten cases it was the pastors who made the allegation, almost all (nine) of witchcraft. However we do not know if the children concerned had been brought to the pastor to confirm or deny prior suspicions of witchcraft held by the parents, as is indicated by the four cases of a joint allegation by parents and pastor.

The cases also showed a rather large number (ten) of apparently single-parent households, almost all headed by women who may have non-resident male partners, but cannot rely on a man's work or salary to support them. In one of them, a girl of 16 complained that her mother said she had an evil spirit. Her father was in the Democratic Republic of Congo, out of communication, and she was expected to help with three small half-siblings, her mother's children by her new partner, who did not

Table 8.3 Accusers of Children

Victim accused of witchcraft by:		Victim said to be possessed by:
Pastor*	9	1*
Mother*	9	7
Stepmother	1	
Called 'mother'	5	
Foster-mother*		1*
Father*	4	4
Stepfather	1	
Relatives	4	3
Member of household	1	
Church members/elders	2	1
Family friend		1
Traffickers	2	
Unclear	1	2

* In four cases pastors acted together with a parent: two mothers, a father and a foster-mother. In some cases there were several accusers.

live with them. Her mother denied making the accusation, but whether the girl was telling the truth about her mother's accusation or not, the bad relationship between mother and child was one that is common in households where conflicts may result in accusations of witchcraft. Although more research is needed to test this suggestion, it does seem as if single parents, like step-parents, may be more likely to be accusers of children whose sole care may seem a heavy burden.

Except for possibly one case, all the accused children have been accused by adults of a senior generation. The case of Kristy Bamu[15] was most unusual in that the killer, Eric Bikubi, accused his partner's brother.[16] With one possible exception, no other London cases involved an accusation between members of the same generation. That case was the case of the Angolan girl, known as 'Child B for legal reasons, who was first accused, according to one witness,[17] by the child of the other woman who lived with her and the woman she called 'mother'. However, the adult members of the household quickly took the matter into their own hands. It was they who attempted to deliver the child and who at one point contemplated murdering her.

The accusers were either members of the same household or pastors to whom the children were taken as suspected witches. Altogether fifty-nine accusations were made against children, whether they were said to be witches (thirty-nine) or possessed by evil spirits (twenty), or sometimes both. Only thirteen accusers were neither members of the same household nor pastors, but of these, seven were the child's relatives and two were elders of a church, so that only four accusations were made by people outside the two contexts of church and family.

In over two-thirds of the cases, the accusation, either of witchcraft or spirit possession, was made against a child by his/her parent, step-parent or classificatory mother. In effect their accusations imply a denial of parenthood in the case of the accused children, who are seen as merely the bodily container for an evil spirit, and no longer a human person. This was made explicit by a woman in Nigeria, whose twin five-year-old boys were found wandering, naked and starving, by journalists making a film. They asked their mother why she had thrown her children out of their home. 'They are not my children,' she answered, 'they are witches'. The evil of witchcraft seems to cancel the duties and responsibilities of parenthood as well as any affection in the relationship.

A surprising finding was the large number of women (sixteen) who made accusations against their own children. One might have expected stepmothers (only one) or classificatory 'mothers' (six) to accuse children with whom they had a difficult relationship without nurturing warmth, but the figures seem to show otherwise. There are various possible reasons for this situation. First there is the observed fact that the records of these cases tend to assimilate all households to the ideal British pattern of the nuclear family, designating adult males as fathers and women as mothers. In some cases it is possible to discover whether these 'parents' are biological parents or not, but in others there may not be any information to go on. Secondly, it is the practice of the authorities to interview mothers about their children, which may account for their predominance in records of the cases. In some cases it is noted that the father agrees with his wife's opinion, but no indication of who was the initiator of their views is given; in others there is no information. As a result one cannot be sure that any of those listed as accusers were the first, or only, accusers of the child witches in the household. But the example of the Nigerian woman given above is a reminder of the depth of conviction felt even by biological mothers. It is quite clear that mothers are as committed to the belief in their children's evil as their fathers and their neighbours.

A few trafficked children are to be found among those accused.[18] They are members of the households of those who accuse them, but their presence is as domestic servants rather than by right of kinship, so they fulfil the criterion of being insecurely placed there. Some Africans seem to think that these are the children most often accused. At one meeting of Nigerian women I attended to talk about my research, a member of the group told me: 'We know about these children. There are rich women who bring in maids and when they don't like them they say they are witches'. This view, however, is not supported by the evidence. As Table 8.3 showed, few accused children have been trafficked. Such evidence as these cases provide suggests that this remark that accused children were trafficked children reflected a common stereotype rather than accurate knowledge, or was deliberately misleading. Among the cases being discussed here, there are only four in which children were clearly trafficked. In the first, a girl aged 16 went to Social Services to complain that she was being treated as a slave: she did not go to school, and worse, she was not taken to the doctor, although she had contracted hepatitis. In the second, two brothers were found to have been trafficked, probably for the second time. Aged 11 and 15 on this occasion, they had been found by the authorities previously, staying with different hosts, and had been returned to Nigeria. Yet they were once more in London living with 'friends of their parents'. Parents may take a payment for handing their child or children to traffickers, but it was not established whether they had on this occasion. In another five cases the interview material raised the suspicion that trafficking was involved, but the adults were not described by the authorities as traffickers, unlike the householders in the two instances described who were actually charged with trafficking.[19]

African parents may 'give' their children to distant relatives or even strangers in the hope of obtaining better education and prospects for them in Britain.[20] Both Victoria Climbié and 'Child B' were brought to England by distant relatives, not their own parents or close kin. As was argued in the case of Victoria, it is very difficult to refuse a senior relative who offers this opportunity and asks for the favour of informally adopting a child. Those who receive a child may pay the parent or professional traffickers for it; in recompense, they claim child benefits and use their free labour as cleaners, shoppers and childminders. More formal, legal adoption of children from Nigeria by Nigerian couples in Britain is becoming more common, according to my informants, although among Nigerians it had previously been regarded negatively, and is still not always successful.

Pastors and Deliverance

A Congolese woman, in response to a question asking why things had changed from the old days when children were not considered capable of witchcraft, responded: 'The pastors told us that it was so'. Indeed an early work written by the Nigerian pastor, Dr D.K. Olukoya, General Overseer of the Mountain of Fire and Miracles, has a section that makes clear that his church believes children can be witches (Olukoya 1999: 152–55).[21]

There are rapidly growing numbers of Pentecostal churches whose pastors are prepared to identify children as witches. The figures support this: as noted earlier in ten cases it was pastors who accused the children, in all but one of the cases of witchcraft and in four other cases they acted together with the adult responsible for the child. Two more accusations were made by church elders.

Given the proliferation of small churches whose pastors are very willing to seek out witches (see Chapter 7) and to deliver them, this figure is probably a minimum one. It is likely that pastors accused children of witchcraft in some other cases as well, but parents either did not mention it or were not asked about it, since there are references to pastors in some statements. For instance, one father was heard by his children saying that 'it was all the fault of the pastor' and two women were recorded as having consulted pastors in Nigeria about the alleged witchcraft of children in their households.[22] The women who looked after both Victoria Climbié and 'Child B' had consulted pastors about their suspicions of the children. Two boys, accused by their pastor father of witchcraft almost as soon as they arrived from Kinshasa to join their parents, had been accused by a pastor there before they left, according to him. In London, pastors may point to children in the congregation at the services they are holding and claim they are witches. The role of pastors was discussed in the last chapter, and the study of cases confirms their very important role in substantiating beliefs in witchcraft and particularly in endorsing the belief in children as evil.

Not all children are taken to pastors for 'diagnosis' and, if they are, not all of them are 'delivered' by the pastor. One mother, faced with two children accused in Kinshasa where they had been left with other church members, reminded her husband that he too was a pastor and could exorcise them, which would cost much less. Her husband, who was labouring to establish his own church in England having failed to find a suitable job, was obviously attracted by the opportunity to demonstrate his spiritual powers to his small congregation. For these and other reasons, many other parents try to deliver their children themselves, using the common methods: fasting, deprivation of water and sleep, beatings and other maltreatments with boiling water and other heated material, all of which are designed to make the evil spirit leave the human body it has chosen to inhabit.

It is mostly in these cases where children do not survive what is done to them in the name of eliminating witchcraft that publicity is given to what happened. However, unknown to the general public, many children are maltreated at home and in the many Pentecostal, charismatic and 're-awakened' churches where pastors make fighting witchcraft the central part of their professional lives. In the course of the fight, children's lives may be destroyed.

It has been argued here that a variety of causes lie behind the accusations that initiated these reports. Similarities and differences with traditional witchcraft are hard to identify as information is usually inadequate to do so. However, there are two phenomena that are new and disturbing: the danger to children from those adults who are supposed to be responsible for them and the fact that witchcraft attacks are now believed to take place within the household. This is not to say that conflicts within households are new; disputes between parents and children, particularly when the latter are adult and have left home, are not uncommon. They do occur, although we do not know whether they are more frequent among migrants, among the newly urbanised or among the few undisturbed rural communities. However, in any location, for parents to consider their child to be practising witchcraft against them is a new and serious result of change in Africa.

Notes

1   There is a tendency in Britain to talk about 'Africans' as if they were a single people with one culture. This is manifestly not so, and if I do generalise about 'Africans' I am aware of the enormity of doing so. Nevertheless there are some common features, and some of those are manifest in beliefs about witchcraft.

2   I did fieldwork among the Gisu in the Eastern Province of Uganda from 1953 to 1955.

3   I published a narrative account of the difficulties I encountered in *Anthropology Today* (La Fontaine 2012).

4   The likelihood of this thinking was pointed out to me by Zoltan Biro at a King's graduate seminar where I read a first draft of a paper on the difficulties of certain types of research in contemporary Britain (La Fontaine 2012).

5   But not entirely; many of the children accused of witchcraft were born in Britain, as were a few of their parents.

6   One head teacher told me that she was sure that parents in her area had decided that two answers to questions about disciplining a child were acceptable to the local authorities: 'We stop them watching TV' or 'We shut them in their rooms'. As she remarked to me, many of these parents were living in small flats where the children all slept in one room and if there was a television, it was in the room where everyone ate and from which it would be difficult to exclude any child. However they produced the stereotypical answers which seem to have been accepted, unfortunately for the children concerned.

7   'The Invisibility of Children' is the title of a collection of papers on this subject edited by Helle Rydstrom and myself. They were given at a seminar at Tema Barn, the Childrens' Research Centre in Linkoping University, Sweden , which published them under that title in 1998.

8   In all of them the police had been involved, and it was from their archive that I obtained the information used.

9   Mrs Thrale kindly gave me a printout recording the cases she found, for which I was most grateful. I found it very helpful in showing me what to look for.

10   I am happy to record my indebtedness to SCD5 who put up with my presence in their office almost daily for several months and helped to find dockets and files for me.

11   Conversations with Thomas Bikebi and Romain Matondo between 1992 and 1994.

12   In Eastern and Southern Africa, accusations made by younger men and women against the elderly have resulted in deaths occasioned by mob violence. In contrast, Ghana's northern territories contain a number of villages (known as camps) where accused witches, mostly elderly women, live out their exile from their homes.

13   In both Tanzania and Uganda, children have been killed or mutilated to provide body parts as ingredients for magic. This indicates a rather different view of children there. In Zambia and Malawi, however, there have been incidents where children were accused of witchcraft.

14   I learnt of this over forty years ago from a neighbour who was undergoing family therapy with her husband and children, but have had it confirmed over the years since. However I am aware that this association might be out of date.

15   This case has not been included in the figures as it began to be reported after I ended the research.

16   Bikubi accused all his partner's siblings to start with, but narrowed his accusations to Kristy who had shown behaviour that might be seen as a sign of witchcraft: he had wet his pants when unable to get into the bathroom.

17   DNA analysis showed her to be a more distant relative.

18   Such children are brought to the U.K. as cheap labour: they work as nurses for younger children, as domestic servants or at other menial tasks, receiving little more than their board and keep. Boys from South East Asia are reported to be being brought in to work in cannabis factories, but the African children seem to be girls more than boys. This may reflect the numbers forced into the sex trade, both in England and, frequently, in Italy.

19   Only one couple was convicted.

20   Esther Goody has written extensively of the Ghanaian practice of sending children to stay with other relatives, either to help them where they are elderly or to benefit from living in a household of higher status. See Goody 1966, 1970, 1974. Similar practices were also recorded in Buganda in East Africa by Audrey Richards – see Richards 1960: 66 for an account of sending boys to live in the households of men of greater wealth and status to give them advantages in an adult career.

21   On the church's website, Dr Olukoya is credited with writing more than seventy 'books', of which seven (Nos 9, 24, 27, 38, 58, 63, 69) concern witchcraft and deliverance.

22   One of these women used to pay her pastor regularly for his advice, using American Express.

Bibliography

de Boeck, F. 2001. 'Garimpero Worlds: Digging, Dying and "Hunting" for Diamonds in Angola', *Review of African Political Economy* 1: 549–562.

———. 2004. 'The Divine Seed: Children, Gift and Witchcraft in the Democratic Republic of Congo', in F. de Boeck and A. Honwana (eds), *Makers and Breakers: Children and Youth in Postcolonial Africa*. Oxford: James Curry, pp. 188–214.

————. 2009. 'At Risk, as Risk: Abandonment and Care in a World of Spiritual Insecurity', in J. La Fontaine (ed.), *The Devil's Children: From Spirit Possession to Witchcraft, New Allegations that Affect Children*. Farnham: Ashgate, pp. 129–150.

Goody, E.N. 1966. 'Fostering in Ghana: A Preliminary Survey', *Ghana Journal of Sociology* 2: 26–33.

————. 1970 . 'Kinship Fostering in Gonja: Deprivation or Advantage?', in P. Mayer (ed.), *Socialisation: The Approach from Social Anthropology*. London: Tavistock, pp.51-74

————. 1974. *Contexts of Kinship*. Cambridge: Cambridge University Press.

Kochan,B. (ed.). 2014. *Migration and London's growth*. London: London School of Economics.

La Fontaine, J.S. 2012. 'Research at Home', *Anthropology Today* 28(5) (October).

Olukoya, D.K. 1999. *Overpowering Witchcraft*. Lagos: Ministry of Fire and Miracles International Headquarters

Paccoud, A. 2014. 'Migrant Trajectories in London: Spreading Wings or Facing Displacement', in B. Kochan (ed.), *Migration and London's Growth*. London: London School of Economics, pp. 27–40.

Pereira, L. 2011. 'Families, Churches, the State and the Child-Witch in Angola', in Luiz Peres and Roger Sansi (eds), *Sorcery in the Black Atlantic*. Chicago: Chicago University Press, pp. 187–209.

Richards, A.I. 1960. 'The Ganda', in A.I. Richards (ed.), *East African Chiefs*. London: Faber, pp. 41–77.

Stobart, E. 2006. 'Child Abuse Linked to Accusations of "Possession" and "Witchcraft"'. Report presented to the (then) Department of Education and Science (DfES).

Thrale (née Spargo), C. 2005. 'Child Abuse Investigation Command: Congolese Ritual Abuse'. Criminal Intelligence Cases from 2000 to April 2005. SCD(10) Intelligence Unit (unpublished).

CONCLUSION
Continuities and Changes

This book challenges the assumption that witchcraft beliefs left no trace in English culture when they were no longer held. The first two chapters presented evidence to the contrary. Building on anthropological discussions of the nature of evil, they argued that in England the ideas and symbols that constitute 'evil' are directly comparable with those of witchcraft. To start with, the conviction that a secret conspiracy exists that threatens ordered society has been manifest in a variety of public alarms (Jenkins 1992; Frankfurter 2006: 7–9) in the many years following the end of the hunt for witches, the most recent and dramatic being the 'satanic panic', which demonstrated most clearly its descent from the historic English belief in witchcraft. The alleged secret rituals of the Devil-worshippers who featured in it closely resembled the Witches' Sabbath, particularly in the distorted images of the Christian mass that were included in both.

In addition, the outrageous acts attributed to Satanists are those that are found in the stereotypical pictures of witches in many other cultures. With the exception of the power to inflict harm on other people, the acts attributed to Satanists are very similar to the practices of witches, as indeed they are to ideas of witchcraft in other societies. Incest, cannibalism, murder, sexual perversions, the infliction of disaster and disease do not all occur together in each and every society's view of witchcraft, but there is a considerable overlap in the acts that make up the various cultural images of that inhuman creature, the night witch. They constitute the witch as inhuman.

What does distinguish the traditional witch beliefs of other societies, together with those of Europe before the witch-hunts, from the modern English concepts of evil is their explanatory function. Western science has different ways of explaining the world from those contained in magic and witchcraft, and they are based on evidence rather than conviction or faith. It is in this context that 'the ... notion of witchcraft is incompatible with our ways of thought' (Evans-Pritchard 1937: 81). This has been shown recently by the Ebola epidemic in West Africa, which is widely believed by communities suffering from it to have been caused by witchcraft. Those who survive may be regarded with suspicion in case they used the witchcraft that had been its cause. In England such unexpected calamities and the common inequities of life are mostly left unexplained or labelled 'accident', 'coincidence' or 'luck' – terms which describe, but do not explain, their occurrence. Although the participants in a secret conspiracy may still be thought to resemble the members of a coven, misfortunes are no longer attributed to the evil magic of enemies in the community or understood as generated by the human emotions of jealousy and malice. Nevertheless, as Pocock (1985) demonstrated, even though we no longer believe in witches, the inexplicable in human behaviour may still be dismissed as 'evil' in a way that differs only in its manner of representation from saying 'It was witchcraft'. As noted above, many of the evil acts characteristic of the former witches still represent inhuman evil.

It has been pointed out by historians that ideas of witches and their activities differed in the different parts of Europe at the time of the witch-hunts (Thomas 1970; Cohn 1970, 1975). The Devil-worshipping image of witches, built up over the centuries, was held more widely in Scotland and on the Continent[1] than in England. Any connection between it and witchcraft as used in interpersonal local conflicts could be largely ignored by most English historians. As was later argued, it was the religious authorities who identified the ancient myth of secret conspiracies with the worship of Satan, not merely to demonise heretics, but to force the uneducated rural communities to abandon their beliefs in, and practices of, all forms of magic, unless they were authorised by the Church, which offered holy relics as well as religious charms that were believed to have the power to heal sufferers and solve their problems. The first studies of witchcraft in early modern Europe had been dominated by English and American scholars, whose views had been determined by their comparison of a special case (England) with African material, that resembled it much more than did any of the witch-beliefs in Europe.[2] As a result, it was argued subsequently that their conclusions were not valid more widely (Ankerloo and Henningsen 1990: introduction). In effect, the suggestion that these explanations were not appropriate for European witchcraft was a charge of ethnocentricity. The collection of essays by European scholars (Ankarloo and Henningsen 1990) focused on the central cases of early modern witch-hunts, comparing them with the peripheral ones that more closely resembled the English equivalents, and concentrating on the wider significance of the witch-hunts. They showed the political dimensions involved, the spread of state control of rural areas, and the manner in which the hunts were started, and stopped.[3] They looked not merely at beliefs, but at the actions of the leaders of the hunt and at the context that provided the motivations of the actors.

Human sacrifice is one of the actions associated with Devil-worshipping witches that is still commonly used as a label for some killings. The discovery by explorers and colonial forces that human sacrifice was actually practised in some societies, such as those of the Incas and of some West African peoples, may have been the reason why this, rather than other features of witchcraft, came to represent all that was savage, backward and uncivilised – that is, it became symbolic of the alien Other. Be that as it may, the label of human sacrifice is often attributed to murders involving members of societies very different from Britain. One such case, much discussed in the media and analysed in detail in Chapter 4, provided an opportunity to demonstrate the misleading nature of ethnocentric interpretations and show how comparisons with similar acts in other cultures can be a more effective way of approaching understanding of apparently inexplicable behaviour. It also showed the difference between magical acts, usually performed in secret to benefit an individual who pays for them, and the public performance of rituals that are undertaken for the good of the community.

The distinction between ritual acts of killing and murder is a significant element of a culture's moral system. Sacrifice took (or takes) place in prescribed ways for culturally justified purposes; judicial executions in Western countries resemble human sacrifice in this respect, although sacrifice is a religious act, while an execution is clearly secular.[4] It may be argued that a reason behind human sacrifice is a disregard for the value of human life, but as has been pointed out in early accounts (see Law 1985), it is the high value of a human, rather than an animal, life given as an offering to gods or ancestral spirits that made human sacrifice the choice in certain rituals.[5] True human sacrifice is relatively rarely found in the twenty-first century, but cases are reported, usually from the remoter areas of India where the cult of the goddess Kali may be claimed to justify it.[6]

One of the mistaken applications of the term 'human sacrifice' to a killing was the subject of Chapter 4. The ensuing discussion also provided an opportunity to distinguish the evil form of magic, also sometimes referred to as 'black magic' or 'sorcery', from witchcraft. Parts of human bodies, sometimes hacked from a living victim, are the ingredients in extreme forms of it. This particularly strong magic was thought to enhance the powers of those individuals who could afford to commission the specialist magicians to supply it. The human ingredients are thought to activate the other elements of the magic and give it extra force. It has frequently been reported in several parts of Africa,[7] notoriously in Tanzania, where people with albinism, including young children and babies, have been killed to provide ingredients for these powerful spells. The discovery of the mutilated body of a child in the Thames has been the only known case of this in Britain and it was immediately labelled 'human sacrifice'. However this killing cannot be identified as a sacrifice unless it fulfils the conditions that define such rituals; in this instance, the context for the death remains unknown.

Historians[8] have shown that healers in early modern Europe also used human body parts, such as blood or the powdered flesh and bones of corpses. The use lingered on in folk medicine,[9] although modern medicine ultimately discarded it as it developed more effective treatment and a more scientific knowledge of human physiology.[10] In the recent African cases we know of, as detailed in the official report by Prof. V. Ralushai (1996), the use of the term *muti*,[11] translatable as medicine, for these deaths and mutilations indicates a significant difference in purpose from sacrifice. It was also different from *muti*. The European uses of human body parts did not include effects that were not physical; unlike the African form it was not believed to promote wealth or good fortune. It is a practice that is secret, not public, offering no tribute to a deity or benefit to the community and it is seen as morally wrong in the communities where it happens. It therefore cannot be described as a religious act. The victim whose body is used has no relation to the person causing this attack and may be quite unknown to him. The link with interpersonal conflict and rivalries that constitutes the explanatory aspect of witchcraft beliefs is not involved either and in some respects, being based on a particular view of human physiology, *muti* is closer to medical science than either witchcraft or religion. As we can now see, it shows how a major misinterpretation can be caused by an ethnocentric judgement which, though common enough in English society, is a pitfall that anthropologists are taught to try to avoid. Comparison based on carefully researched ethnographic evidence is still the best way of explaining acts which are alien to English practices.

Continuity and Change

The persistence of witchcraft beliefs among members of many Third World societies, both in their native countries and as migrants in the countries of others, is seen by many Westerners as clear evidence that such peoples cling to their traditional (and uncivilised) beliefs. Reports of the lynching of accused witches in Papua New Guinea, India and Africa, resembling all too closely the witch-hunts of early modern Europe, are publicised in news reports. Witch-hunts across the world are taken to demonstrate the strength of these convictions, and their primitive nature, by the brutality of the actions they trigger. They are easily misinterpreted as indications of a stage of development that lags behind that of Europe. Accusations of witchcraft against children that have resulted in the abuse and even death of the accused are wrongly attributed to traditions that persist even when believers are living among those of another culture. Paradoxically then, residents in the First World are thought to have slowly abandoned beliefs through social changes that took place over several centuries while denizens of the Third have persisted in retaining similar ideas throughout the most radical and rapid social transformations.

That there is continuity with the past in England has been amply demonstrated. It may take the form of concepts of evil that incorporate much of the content of witch beliefs or erupt in public panics about hidden conspiracies. As far as the first is concerned, the parallel with the image of the witch is close: the occasional evil act committed for intelligible if culpable reasons, like the occasional use of witchcraft, may be contrasted with the permanent evil nature of some human beings, who resemble night witches in that their behaviour cannot be explained or condoned. The stereotype of 'the paedophile' is a current example of the latter. Research into the rash of accusations of ritual abuse or Satanism at the end of the twentieth century has shown that the cause of what became known as the Satanic Panic, or the Satanism Scare, was not merely the conviction that the millennium was approaching, as held by some Christians of the new denominations. It was also one manifestation of the persistent belief in evil conspiracies that have been shown to characterise the culture of at least some sections of English society (see Chapter 2).

Yet beliefs in witchcraft, like any other beliefs, may change over time and there is clear evidence that they have done so. In Britain the addition of 'child sexual abuse' to features of 'satanic rituals' reflects a more modern form of incest that has become a real social evil; its inclusion in the 'satanic rituals' draws on the actuality of reported cases to support the unsubstantiated allegations of other aspects of the alleged 'Devil-worship' (see also La Fontaine 1998). The victims of modern evil-doers in England are seen as children who are abused, injured or even killed.

By contrast, in parts of Africa, children are no longer merely the victims of witchcraft; now they may be believed to be witches themselves. In the past these African children were regarded as too weak and ignorant to perform witchcraft; accusing them of it is one major change in these beliefs. In other societies children may be included with their mother in a joint accusation, as they were in early modern Europe; these African children are now accused as separate individuals. Such changes seem to have been set in motion by new concepts of childhood stemming from the observation of street children, child soldiers and abandoned children who have survived without adult support. The context for these changes is a variety of disasters, both man-made and natural, such as the results of civil war and epidemics such as AIDS. Orphan children have managed to survive in the street and some have even made more money than adults in a variety of types of earnings, or have acquired firepower as soldiers. These factors have had the effect of changing adult views of them; they may seem as independent, even powerful – but also, like adults, capable of evil.[12]

As has been argued in Chapter 6, tradition alone is not to blame; nor is the context. The new accusations against children show the influence of Pentecostal and other charismatic forms of evangelical Christianity and their integration into local cosmologies. The preaching of war against evil and sin and the declarations of the need to fight against the activities of Satan and the spirits who serve him, emphasise the fundamentalist doctrines of the new Pentecostal churches. In many parts of the world now, being a witch may entail being thought to be possessed by a spirit, one of Satan's servants and followers. This is the other major change in ideas of witches. It is the satanic spirit that endows a person with the power to harm others with witchcraft; and to fight against it, God's gift of exorcism to deliver the possessed one is granted to pastors. The exorcism of these spirits eliminates the source of witchcraft's power, something that could not be achieved according to traditional practices. The current understanding, justifying the violence used in exorcising or, as they say delivering, the accused, differs markedly from that of precolonial Africa, and indeed of early modern Europe. Nevertheless the results are often similar to those that once killed and wounded suspected witches in many parts of the world. The involvement of pastors in accusations of witchcraft was clear in many cases of London's witch children discussed in Chapter 8. It is these pastors, whose existence exemplifies the Christianisation of Africa, who are its witch-finders now, not the magicians and diviners of a traditional past.

Nevertheless these changes have not eradicated some significant differences between the moral frameworks of England and those of these other societies in which witchcraft is still believed. The basis of evil action in traditional English belief is the conspiring group, meeting in secret, whose ultimate ambition is to destroy Christianity and the whole social world of its adherents. It is the mirror image of church congregations or of a responsible gathering of citizens to ensure the well-being of the community. By contrast, in other societies evil is usually represented by the individual witch, who is anti-social, not wholly human and who rejoices in malice for its own sake, not as part of a longer term aim. In modern Christian communities in Africa, what is to be feared is still the evil of individuals rather than the conspiracies of groups.[13]

The position of children relative to the different perceptions of evil is also one of contrast. In England and large parts of Africa, children are still considered victims: of devil-worshippers or other evil-doers. The alleged accounts of ritual abuse at the end of the twentieth century were said to show that children might reveal the truth of what was happening; Believe the Children was a popular rallying cry for campaigners. As this chapter was being completed, there have been reports of the trial of a man whose children were coerced, violently, into accusing him of satanistic sexual crimes against them by their mother and her new partner. In contrast, one major change that characterises the modern African beliefs lies in the new vulnerability of children to accusations of being perpetrators instead of the victims of accusations of witchcraft.

Changes in the position of children, in the West as well as in Africa, have been encouraged by the fundamentalist revival of the concept of Original Sin, particularly evident among some Pentecostal Christians in the United States. Their views of child-rearing, such as that pain is of positive advantage for purifying children and frequent beating is a necessity if children are to become good Christian adults, have been well documented. The damaging effects on American children of this kind of upbringing have been pointed out by a number of writers.[14] The deaths of children who are thought to be possessed of evil spirits may occur without allegations of witchcraft among these American revivalist Christians, but they are not dissimilar to the deaths of child-witches in Africa. In fact, to the outside observer, children subjected to this Christian violence are as much victims as those who are accused of witchcraft elsewhere.

It has been argued, cogently, that wars, famines, epidemics and forced migrations in Africa have created an atmosphere that encourages allegations of witchcraft against adults as well as children. The observation that children may survive without parental care is a consequence of these disasters, both the natural and the man-made.[15] In Africa, the traditional valuation of children as forms of wealth is giving way to a different view of them: as responsibilities. Their value may also have declined, as poverty and social disturbances necessitating migration make their upbringing increasingly burdensome and their labour in agriculture unnecessary. Like the elderly women pursued as witches by lynch mobs or burnt to death in both past and present witch-hunts, children may be considered dispensable.[16] Moreover the experiences of many children may leave them traumatised and unruly; these are some of the 'difficult' children who are likely to be accused. Similarly, English children in poor urban districts are also likely to appear out of control and disorderly; reports of their involvement in crimes such as the distribution of drugs, theft and muggings, as well as prostitution and gang warfare, are matters of public concern. Legal orders that may confine such children to their homes after school hours are one English reaction to the problem.

Understanding witchcraft entails the consideration of sets of ideas, but they must be seen within the social context that their concepts inform and are informed by. Actions and relationships in which the ideas are worked out in practice are vital elements of this system as it operates in daily life. Historical events that may add new factors must also be considered. There is one other factor that must not be forgotten: the existence of individuals who promote ideas that stimulate action in others. In the case of London, the activities of those who encourage individuals to believe in witchcraft and to accuse others of it are part of the whole picture. Detailed studies by modern historians such as Gustav Henningsen[17] show the effects of these 'witch-finders' in the past. Some of them, while not wholly responsible for the accusations and trials with which they have been associated, undoubtedly encouraged the popular wish to rid itself of witches. Similarly, the pastor of an African independent church in London said to me that although there were too many witches in Africa to get rid of them all, here in London there was a chance to cleanse the place completely. This was his goal, and that of many of his colleagues.

Of course the successful stimulation of witch-finding activities requires the pre-existence of fears and tensions in the local population as well as the relevant beliefs, but in many instances charismatic individuals undoubtedly focused popular concerns and encouraged the hunt for witches. Lynch mobs, too, may be triggered by individuals. The witch-hunts in Africa in the last century were in good measure the work of anti-witchcraft crusaders (see Richards 1935; Marwick 1950; Redmayne 1970; Willis 1970); today the founders and pastors of Independent African Churches fill that role. Like the early witch-finders, they are encouraged by the popular acclaim they earn. The analysis in Chapter 7, and the evidence of their involvement in actual cases, has shown that it is their competition for followers that has resulted in the increase – not merely in the size of their congregations, but in the numbers of accusations of witchcraft levelled against children as the unintended consequence of this rivalry.

This combination of belief and action in a particular social and historical setting generates the actual witchcraft accusations that form the data for further research and further understanding of these consequences. The cases of London's witch children (Chapter 8) revealed some major changes in relationships, particularly those between parents and children. The recorded accusations in London cases showed children accused by their parents or step-parents. These accusations are the opposite of traditional ones in which the witches were believed to harm children in order to attack their parents. Now some parents may injure and even kill their own children if they believe them to be the witches who are their enemies. This absence of responsible care and affection that is expected in parents can also be observed in the child abuse revealed in some English households. The comparison indicates that it is not only the presence or absence of witchcraft beliefs that causes these atypical events, despite the existence of fundamentalist Christian theology, crusading pastors or violent exorcism. It is more likely that they reflect a combination of all these.

Whether they are prefaced by witchcraft claims or not, it is very difficult to discover the incidence of harm to children in urban settings, unless the violence is extreme. The emphasis on privacy in domestic life in Western societies, together with architecture that excludes outsiders more effectively than the more permeable material of houses in other societies, makes any maltreatment of children relatively unnoticeable to outsiders. Neighbours and even professional child protection workers may remain unaware until it is too late. Whether witchcraft accusations that do not come to the notice of the authorities are also those that are less extreme and whether they show the same symptoms of deteriorated relationships within the household as those that are reported, are matters for future research. We need to know much more about the generation of evil before we can prevent it.

Notes

1 One could use the term 'Continental Witchcraft to denote this belief in the witch as Devil-worshipper that was promulgated as the result of proselytising by clerical witch-hunters. Thus the images described in the 'satanic panic' resembled Continental rather than the kind of English witchcraft that had been discussed.

2 Note Keith Thomas's statement, in his article on the use of anthropology, that he proposes to omit the theological development of witch beliefs as they were not important in England (1970: 49).

3 An excellent example of this is Henningsen 1980 (cf. Macfarlane 1970a, 1970b; Thomas 1971).

4 Nor is it often recognised that the Roman invaders of Britain were appalled by the human sacrifices they discovered among the local (British) tribes; they forbade the practice in the areas they controlled.

5 One of the readers of my manuscript reminded me of this, and I am happy to acknowledge this here.

6 A dozen reports of offerings of human sacrifice to the goddess Kali by her devotees, mainly in remote parts of central India, have been reported in the press over the last ten years. I owe this information to Inform, a charity that collects and makes available neutral information on other religions. Their material included a report in the *Boston*

Globe in November 2003 that the *Hindustan Times* had claimed twenty-five cases in six months, but there was no indication of what evidence, if any, had been included in the report they quoted.

7   It was originally reported from South Africa but has been documented in many other African countries. It is less known in West Africa, although I have been told its practice is spreading in Nigeria.

8   A recent example is the monograph by Richard Sugg published in 2011.

9   Of course, modern medicine still uses human blood in transfusions, but in the past the blood was drunk.

10 See the references for Chapter 4. I note that the conclusions I reached in that chapter were my own and not attributable to Dr R. Sugg.

11 This Zulu term is widely used in South Africa for concoctions made by magicians and has been taken over as a label for these killings as well, although many of those who use it clearly do not understand its implications.

12 Prof. Filip de Boeck (2001), who first reported research on these children, has emphasised the significance of a changed view of children in making them vulnerable to accusations of witchcraft.

13 This remark ignores the terror being inflicted by fanatic Muslim groups in Nigeria (Boko Haram) and Kenya (al Shabaab), but they are far from secret conspiracies though their strikes are unexpected and apparently random.

14 For example, see Heimlich 2011. She cites various works in confirmation of her claim that the doctrine is dangerous to children.

15 See the works by de Boeck I have cited in various chapters.

16 I owe this insight to Amanda Sackur.

17 See his fascinating account of the course of an outbreak of allegations of witchcraft in the Basque country in the early seventeenth century (Henningsen 1980). Macfarlane, in his study of witchcraft in Essex, argues that the witch-finders Hopkins and Stearne were wrongly attributed with responsibility for the witch-hunts there (Macfarlane 1970: 138–40). Probably the situation varied from place to place.

Bibliography

Ankarloo, B., and G. Henningsen (eds). 1990. *Early Modern European Witchcraft: Centres and Peripheries*. Oxford: Clarendon.

Cohn, N. 1970. 'The Myth of Satan and his Human Servants', in M. Douglas (ed.), *Witchcraft Confessions and Accusations*. London: Tavistock, pp. 47–80.

———. 1975. *Europe's Inner Demons*. London: Paladin.

De Boeck, F. 2001. 'Garimpeiro Worlds: Digging, Dying and Hunting for Diamonds in Angola', *Review of African Political Economy* 28(90): 549–562.

Evans-Pritchard, E.E. 1937. *Witchcraft, Oracles and Magic among the Azande*. Oxford: Clarendon Press.

Frankfurter, D. 2006. *Evil Incarnate: Rumors of Demonic Conspiracy and Satanic Abuse in History*. Princeton, NJ: Princeton University Press.

Heimlich, J. 2011. *Breaking Their Will: Shedding Light on Religious Child Maltreatment*. Amherst, NY: Prometheus Books.

Henningsen, G. 1980. *The Witches' Advocate: Basque Witchcraft and the Spanish Inquisition.* Reno: University of Nevada Press.

Jenkins, P. 1992. *Intimate Enemies: Moral Panics in Great Britain.* New York: Walter de Gruyter.

La Fontaine, J. 1998. *Speak of the Devil.* Cambridge: Cambridge University Press.

Law, R. 1985. 'Human Sacrifice in Pre-Colonial West Africa', *African Affairs* 84(334) (January): 53–58.

Macfarlane, A. 1970a. *Witchcraft in Tudor and Stuart England: A Comparative and Regional Study.* London: Routledge & Kegan Paul.

———. 1970b. 'Witchcraft in Tudor and Stuart Essex', in M. Douglas (ed.), *Witchcraft: Confessions and Accusations.* London: Tavistock, pp. 81–102.

Marwick, M. 1950. 'Another Modern Anti-witchcraft Movement in East Central Africa', *Africa* xx(2): 100–112.

Pocock, D. 1985. 'Unruly Evil', in D. Parkin (ed.), *The Anthropology of Evil.* Oxford: Basil Blackwell, pp. 42–56.

Ralushai, N.V. 1996. 'Report of the Commission of Enquiry into Witchcraft, Violence and Ritual Murders in the Northern Province of the Republic of South Africa'. Unpublished manuscript.

Redmayne, A. 1970. 'Chikanga: An African Diviner with an International Reputation', in M. Douglas (ed.), *Witchcraft Confessions and Accusations.* London: Tavistock, pp. 103–128.

Richards, A.I. 1935. 'A Modern Movement of Witchfinders', *Africa* 8(4): 448–461.

Sugg, R. 2011. *Mummies, Cannibals and Vampires: The History of Corpse Medicine from the Renaissance to the Victorians.* London and New York: Routledge.

Thomas, K. 1970. 'The Relevance of Anthropology to the Historical Study of English Witchcraft', in M. Douglas (ed.), *Witchcraft Confessions and Accusations.* London: Tavistock, pp. 47–80.

———. 1971. *Religion and the Decline of Magic.* London: Weidenfeld & Nicholson.

Willis, R. 1970. 'Instant Millennium: The Sociology of African Witch-cleansing Cults', in M. Douglas (ed.), *Witchcraft Confessions and Accusations.* London: Tavistock, pp. 129–140.

INDEX

Lightning Source UK Ltd.
Milton Keynes UK
UKOW01f0652050917
308612UK00015B/1025/P